Menu

CONTENT

Apéritif

"A woman is a fountain, a source, a wellspring that nourishes the world around her. Her lover or spouse, family, friends, professional associates and community, all draw from her fullness. But how does she replenish and empower this fullness?"

Hors D'oeuvres: Where You've Been & Where You Want to Go

There are plenty of how to books available for getting married, dealing with the legal and financial aspects associated with getting a divorce, how to raise kids, and how to process grief. There are financial planners, therapists and real estate agents targeting divorcés, as well as many support groups available. Yet, despite the continued high divorce rate and multitude of people like yourself starting their lives over post divorce, becoming empty nesters or widowed, few resources are available that serve up a saucy action plan for starting over in all areas, particularly in our relationships.

The purpose of this book is to help you redesign your life in an irresistible way. You'll find specific tools from which to pick and choose. They've been designed to assist you in exploring the depths of your being, and to release what no longer serves. Included are resources to help you make new, healthy relationship and life choices.

Recipe for Paying Attention

- You still love one another, but no longer share interests.
- The sexual chemistry that brought you together has waned such that you now prefer to sleep in the guest room.
- The annoying habits you've tolerated under the umbrella of your commitment now irritate you.
- You find yourself staying away from the house longer to avoid confrontation.
- You get frustrated easily and notice you're no longer the kind self you were during those romantic years.
- The crooked teeth you once found endearing are now a major turn off.
- You have judgments about your partner's spending habits.
- You feel threatened by how your partner looks appraisingly at attractive people, yet are afraid to say anything.
- You find yourself (or your partner) drinking or smoking to excess rather than having "those conversations".
- You don't respect how your partner is raising (or have raised) their children - or yours!
- You are exhausted due to your partner snoring, and don't know how to address the issue since "they can't help it".
- You don't like the way your partner dresses yet don't know how to broach the subject.
- When you got together your partner was in great physical shape. Now, they've become lazy, heavy, and you find yourself no longer turned on.
- The kids have left and you realize you no longer know the person to whom you're married, and are not inspired to do anything about it.
- You're completely bored in bed, yet don't want to hurt your partner by having an affair.

Peppered throughout are many anecdotes from friends and clients undergoing their transformational journeys.

If you're in partnership, have the desire to stay together, but are bored, frustrated or simply resigned that nothing can change, you still can juice it up before quitting. You'll feel better if you've given it everything before going separate ways. After all, the stakes are high!

Each section is designed to help you tap into the courage it takes to pay attention, recognize signposts that alert you to make changes, acknowledge what has and hasn't worked, slice and dice dysfunctional patterns, and master specific communication tools. By the end, you'll be standing in front of the perfect smorgasbord for creating a new, irresistible life - one as big as you dare to envision.

Why a New Recipe Helps

Old friends and new have commented on the extraordinary job I've done starting my life over. Honestly, it was the most challenging transition I've encountered.

Now it's your turn... there's work to be done!

When I married for the first time in 1998 at the age of 42, I was completely clear that Billy was my one and only husband. Having had two previous marriages, he called me his third and final.

It was 2004. Billy and I had all the ingredients for a happy life in the country. We'd just completed a substantial remodel on our West Sonoma County home. It was nestled in the heart of eleven acres of redwoods, complete with a glorious pool, hot tub, gardens and fruit trees. We were semi-retired, living extraordinary lives filled with wonderful friends and international travel. In addition to pool parties, we hosted fundraising events and women's retreats. We had many commonalities, a wonderful community and a great lifestyle. I had the security, both emotional and financial that I'd wanted.

Yet peeking out from behind the veneer, there was a consistent nudge, a gnawing inside that there might be more. Though Billy was a wonderful man, I consistently felt disappointed. Somehow, the heart connection was missing.

So one night as we were soaking in our hot tub Billy said, "You've been mad at me for ten years and I owe you an apology. You would have been a great mom. But I was clear that I didn't want more kids, having raised my two grown sons. Not having clarity about your desires at the time, you went along with mine."

He was right, with one exception... it wasn't Billy I'd been mad at, but myself. In that moment I realized I'd compromised one of life's biggest gifts, that of being a mother. Instead, I'd settled for a connection with a wonderful man. My choices had consequences. It was the lack of clarity that cost me rather than that I didn't have children.

At that point, my child bearing years had past. Our lives felt rich and full, so we committed to making our marriage work. We found a therapist, studied with relationship experts such as David Deida and learned about tantra from Margot Anand and the Muirs. We invested in extensive coursework at Lafayette Morehouse, where we studied advanced sexuality and mastered how to communicate our upsets in a responsible manner, sharing anything and everything. We always held one another in high regard.

Yet, after giving our partnership everything we could, we chose to part ways.

When we sold our home and separated, nothing felt familiar. Our belongings were in storage, cats with a friend, and no wedding ring. There was no clue how to begin the reinvention process. Identifying as a wife, a homeowner, an integral part of West Sonoma County's vibrant community and living a wealthy lifestyle was over. Though it had been a long time coming, and we were parting as friends, the transition was shocking.

"When you're racing on a sailboat, heading up into the wind, sails winched in - and suddenly the wind changes and your sails start flapping, it's a drag! While you're disappointed that you're no longer in the lead, it's important to get back on course. The faster you trim the sails the better."
~ Barry Morguelan, M.D.; Energy for Success

I landed in the embrace of long-term friends in Marin County. Living communally provided built-in connections for daily life. This took the edge off the grief, but because most of residents were settled in long-term marriages, they were unable to relate. It was clear I needed to create a new identity.

"Karen moved because she couldn't source her new life with her feet in the old one."
~ Fay Freed, Life Design Coach and Guide, and dear friend

Fay was right. It made sense to relocate to place where a new identity could be forged. The question was, to where? After living such a multi-dimensional life in the gorgeous Bay Area, surrounded by like-minded friends with shared values, it was a challenge to find another area that measured up to such high standards. Though four distinct seasons are wonderful, and being near my family in New England held appeal, the twenty-five winters spent there early in life crossed the North East off the list. The South and Midwest weren't a consideration, as no friends or family beckoned. Since the

Recipe for Emotional Support

Part of starting over is having ways to process the grief resulting from what you've left behind. Here's a list of some support options for you:

- ▶ Hire a psychologist or therapist.

- ▶ Find someone to guide you in a rebirth or breathing experience.

- ▶ Join a grief support group (try MeetUp.com or Facebook for resources).

- ▶ Meditate. Get quiet, Do whatever it takes to quiet your mind enough to allow clear thoughts to emerge from the chaos inherent to big changes.

- ▶ Spend time in nature. Walk on the beach. Go swimming. Go hiking. Go camping.

- ▶ Take a trip! Changing the channel of your reality can be refreshing.

- ▶ Spend time with close friends or family.

- ▶ Keep a journal. Note your observations, thoughts and feelings. Write goals big and small, and especially take time to acknowledge all the good in your life.

- ▶ Ask a good friend to be your sounding board. Request candid feedback.

cold nights and mornings of Northern California summers were never my favorite, Southern California held allure.

A few exploratory road trips revealed San Diego, with the warmer ocean and air, as an irresistible place to start over. Moreover, I had recently established a deep connection with 'Shelli', a new girlfriend introduced by a Bay Area friend. Together, she helped me find a lovely apartment with an ocean view.

After four years living in community with friends in Marin County, it was compelling to create a home for myself. Two friends, my car and the moving van transported me to the apartment I'd call home for the next two years. When everything was hung on the walls and boxes broken down, my friends who helped returned to San Francisco. Finding myself five hundred miles south of the place I'd called home left me more alone than ever. Exploring my new neighborhood and networking for my consulting business provided a little distraction. I joined several online dating sites and met a few nice guys. But at the end of the day, it was just me; feeling lost and alone.

This was definitely an existential crisis. So many questions swirled in my head:

- Who was I without the husband and the ring on my finger?
- Who was I now that the lovely home on eleven acres in Sonoma County belonged to someone else?
- Who was I no longer surrounded by and buoyed by my circle of friends, many of whom I'd known for more than two decades?
- Who was this person that was completely dependent upon GPS to get from one destination to another?

Like the little green cartoon character Gumby, my feet were in one place, while the rest of my body felt stretched elsewhere.

Yesterday's footsteps were still in the Bay Area, yet my bare soles were now walking the beaches of San Diego. Very confusing! Walks on the beach, regular yoga classes and frequent SOS calls home to dear girlfriends helped me stay grounded, as did my participation with the Energy for Success work taught by Dr. Barry Morguelan. My new life depended upon taking the actions necessary to feel home again.

Though it was tempting to stay curled up on the couch eating tiramisu and binging on Netflix, I knew isolating was exactly what I should NOT do. So, chanting a mantra I learned in a personal development training in the '80's, "Oh what the f*%k, go for it anyway", I metaphorically grabbed myself by the lapels and got myself up and out the door. I attended MeetUp groups ranging from business networking to full moon beach parties, to a day's ski trip to Big Bear, to afternoon bowling for people over 50 (where I was the youngest attendee by about a decade), tantra gatherings; basically anything I heard about that might result in my feeling more connected.

It was quite a research project and it gleaned much desired results. I was happy to learn about Hera Hub, which is a collaborative women's office space with U.S. as well as international locations. Lucky for me, one of their three San Diego County locations was less than a five minute drive from my apartment. Hera Hub continues to provide a grounding place to work where I now have many friends and acquaintances.

Soup: The Courage to Change, Ordering Something Different

"Courage doesn't always roar. Sometimes courage is the little voice at the end of the day that says I'll try again tomorrow." ~Mary Anne Radmacher

Change is constant and inevitable. It's one of the only things we can count on in life. Every so often an event occurs that causes significant change, potentially altering our lives completely.

Many things can literally send you to what feels like another planet, including; health crisis, marriage, divorce, death of a loved one, a new job, and moving into a new home. Whether we view the change as good or bad, change is stressful. In response, we might drink too much, rear end an innocent little old lady, or find ourselves in a tearful heap on the living room floor. What matters is your ability to respond to change in a constructive, rather than destructive manner.

"All great changes are preceded by chaos."
~Deepak Chopra

Pay Attention to What's Being Served

First, before changes can be made, you have to pay attention! If you do, you'll usually notice warning signs early enough to respond with necessary actions when it's still easy. Waiting for a crisis is what we did in the past, but not anymore!

"Chronic dissatisfaction is how you sense that you are living a lie."
~David Deida

So... if you're paying attention, I'm going to tell you a very relevant story about the consequences of not paying attention.

My friend Sue and I spent over six weeks driving from Vermont to San Francisco in 1982. Our itinerary was based on wherever friends and family invited us. A few weeks into our trip I felt a twinge in a molar whenever I drank something cold. Though a bit annoying, it wasn't debilitating. It could be

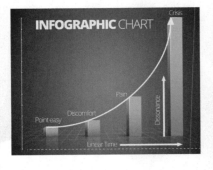

avoided by leaving out the ice. After a few days, hot drinks began to have the same effect. Finding a dentist passed through my mind, but the discomfort was only at a four on a scale of ten. As we traveled west, the discomfort escalated until even biting down became intolerable.

By the time we reached San Francisco, the pain had reached Point Crisis. It was agonizing, off the charts pain, requiring an emergency double root canal to the tune of my last $1500!

If I'd truly paid attention at the "point easy" twinge, I might have found a dentist en route, and had a filling for under $100. Instead, I found myself in crisis.

Can you think of a time when 'not paying attention' led to a poor decision?

Change occurs in subtle ways over time, so paying attention is important. This is why taking periodic inventory of how your life and relationships are going makes sense. Sometimes we're caught by surprise, and find ourselves shocked by changes that might have been prevented, or at least preempted, had we truly been paying attention to clues along the way.

When a client tells me about their spouse's affair, one of the first questions I ask is "When did you first notice a change in your relationship?" Or, at times I just bluntly ask, "When did you stop paying attention such that your partner sought intimacy outside your relationship?"

The unwillingness to pay attention and take preemptive action can be costly. Not only did the toothache cause weeks of discomfort, but Sue had to endure complaints throughout most of the trip.

Of course this story translates to paying attention in all areas of our lives.

~ Carol, age 55, divorced and dating

"I am really hurt that after two months of us being lovers Steve broke up with me with no notice. He took me to dinner over which we had a great conversation with lots of laughs. When we got back to my house he told me our relationship was simply not working for him, and he left. I am so sad!"

When queried about if there were any hints leading up to him breaking it off so suddenly, she shook her head, with a puzzled look on her face. Then, in response to the question, "How were you feeling about him and the relationship?" Carol replied, "He's pretty boring and not up to much in the world compared to the big events I organize and the cool colleagues with whom I'm involved."

There was no response to the next question: "Might he have been responding to your cues perfectly?"

People can be attached to how things have been or how they think they should be, rather than remaining tuned to what is actually occurring. Many times people choose security and familiarity rather than risk the possibility of being alone. Fantasy bonds are formed.

"The fantasy bond acts as a painkiller that cuts off feeling responses and interferes with the development of a true sense of self, and the more a person comes to rely on fantasies of connection, the less he or she will seek or be able to accept love and affection in a real relationship." ~ Wikipedia

Fantasy bonds are usually triggered by incomplete childhood issues. An example is when the daughter of an alcoholic and abusive father might find herself with a husband who has similar dysfunctional traits. If you suspect this might be an issue for you, it's recommended you seek professional assistance to work through childhood wounds.

Taking action when there are warning lights on your dashboard, having regular medical and dental check ups, owning insurance policies for our bodies, cars and homes, are preemptive practices we all use. A warning light or a toothache might alert you to taking care of a minor issue, preventing something worse. Observing, becoming aware of warning signs and taking action gives us the opportunity to avoid drama and disaster, particularly in our relationships.

"Your life does not get better by chance, it gets better by change."
~Jim Rohn

Are you concerned that if you say what you're feeling you'll find yourself way outside your comfort zone, risking your partner's anger or disappointment?

Sometimes it's our partners' smallest habits that can bug us the most! These small issues, if not addressed, can escalate into bigger ones that result in irreparable fissures, leading to a breakup or divorce.

"Sometimes good things fall apart so better things can fall together." ~Marilyn Monroe

~ Laura, age 64, divorced for 12 years, dating.

"The past few times my boyfriend Jim and I got together, and it was time to go to bed, I found myself making up excuses such as needing a snack, or wanting to read something. I blamed my lack of interest on menopause. But when I really thought about it, I knew this was a smokescreen covering up my not being attracted to him any more. The little idiosyncrasies I used to find endearing about Jim had started to bug me. But we had so many good times together! After putting it off, I finally got up the guts to tell him how I was feeling before I found myself acting unkind, or even mean to Jim. We decided to break off the sensual part of our relationship, and though he would prefer us to still be lovers, I'm clear about what I want. At least we've managed to preserve our friendship!"

Unlike Laura and Jim, most people settle for stability and familiarity rather than taking inventory of the "signs", followed by doing what it takes to make tremendous changes. This is relatable for many of us! I know it was nine years from the first indication that things weren't as they seemed before I finally listened to my unhappiness and let my heart guide me.

Just as the frog doesn't recognize the water beginning to boil, the veil of denial can obscure the signs that your relationship might no longer be the one you thought it was.

"Getting over a painful experience is much like crossing monkey bars. You have to let go at some point in order to move forward."
  ~C.S. Lewis

Is it time for you to trust the message your unhappiness and tears are telling you?

~Sarah, married for 15 years, business owner now divorced single mother with half time custody of 16 year old:

"Looking back, I knew it wasn't safe to be around my husband almost ten years before I left him. My daughter, now 16, was just 18 months old. Having missed her nap, she was crying as I prepared dinner. Bob came in the kitchen and asked me a question. When he didn't like my response, he threw a plate against the wall.

That was the first of many episodes in which he lost his temper. Yet I stayed. He was charming and handsome and we had a good sex life. We had a lot of good times, and I especially loved our family life. It wasn't until a friend pointed out that his erratic behaviors were not okay, and that I was actually in danger did I wake up. While my friend was with us, he and I got into a fight. He pushed me really hard causing a severe cut on my head. Having someone there gave me the perspective and courage to finally leave. I'm sad it took me nine years from that first episode."

~Tanya, age 58, divorced after 14 years of marriage:

"There were a few warning signs right from the beginning. Our sex life wasn't good—but I married him anyway because the spiritual component was so strong. I let that override other aspects that ultimately became our demise. Right from the beginning he was very critical of me. It was his way or the highway, He simply over-road me, implying that my approach wasn't as valuable as his. The first time he came down from San Francisco to San Diego for the weekend I was going to re-stain my deck. It took a huge argument about what color stain to buy for me to finally get to have it my way—and it was my house!"

When did you first have an inkling your partner might not be right for you?

~Jessica, Age 39, married for 14 years, divorced for 2 years:

"We were at an airport en route to our engagement party. When the plane was delayed due to bad weather, my fiancée had a tantrum, screaming at one of the gate agents. I knew in that moment I was making a mistake; that my husband to be was not the stable, mature man I'd hoped to be marrying. But I was only 20, had had a very sheltered childhood, and didn't think I had any choice. So we were married, and sure enough, the abuse patterns started soon after. We stayed married for eleven years, during which I spent much of my time frightened that he'd hurt me. I was so lost and miserable that I attempted suicide requiring an induced coma and major surgery. I wonder how things might have been different if I'd had the support of a coach or counselor who pointed out where I had not been paying attention?"

Notice the common retrospective theme. Each woman had known years before they finally took action that their partnership wasn't right for them.

"Daring greatly means the courage to be vulnerable. It means to show up and be seen. To ask for what you need. To talk about how you're feeling. To have the hard conversations." ~Brene Brown, PhD, LMSW

Whetting Your Appetite

Have you ever thought, 'Wow... I'm only 50 +/- years old, have decades of life ahead and would love to be having more fun'?

Maybe you've already gone to a marriage counselor, taken tantra sexuality classes, or even tried alternative relationship styles. Yet still, you're not feeling inspired with your partner. Despite all the warning signs, the dwindling flame, you stay together - kids, extended family and social circles, pets, your home, combined resources including salaries, joint bank accounts, vacations, and the commitment "Til death due us part".

Perhaps you've thought, 'Neither of us are getting LESS wrinkles, so why bother starting over?'

Juice Up Your Relationship

Let's face it... none of us are getting younger! The exciting hormone driven chemistry between you and your partner may have worn off long ago. In its place is a comfortable, cozy connection, but no longer much passion. Yet you'd like to stay together, but not at the expense of your sensuality and sex lives! It's time to do some 'research'. If you try something that works out well, it's great research. You'll do it again. If something doesn't work out, it's also great research—you simply won't repeat it!

Recipe for Enhancing Your Passion

▶ Go to a bookstore or browse through Amazon for books on sexuality and relationship. What appeals to you?

▶ Read sexy stories to one another.

▶ Learn about your anatomy and what feels good to you.

▶ Take a tantra sexuality class (check them out on MeetUp.com)

▶ Watch sexy videos together

▶ Have special date nights with your partner

▶ If intrigued, and it works for both of you, check out alternative lifestyles.

▶ Remember – this is important research! If something doesn't work for you, it's good research, and, if it does work it's good research!

Half Entrées: When There's a Charge to Split Portions

The moment when my husband Billy and I sat on the floor of our empty bedroom holding one another, sobbing, is imprinted in my mind. We were walking away from the beloved home and property that had nourished us for over a decade. Our respective lives, and our lives together were about to change. The pool, sauna, hot tub, walking paths, redwoods, streams, deer, gardens of gorgeous lilies, tulips, and dahlias and roses would now belong to someone else. All this had come to an end, and it was devastating.

Although we made a conscious choice to end our marriage, and did so amicably, the contextual change was tremendous.

Definition of context - The interrelated conditions in which something exists or occurs.

How we perceive things, the context, or world we live in provides the framework of our behaviors. The values we learn from our families, schools, and religious affiliations combine to create our view of reality. Our values and limitations are determined by everything that influenced and conditioned us.

Think of a blind person seeing for the first time. Suddenly, after living in a world of blackness, void of colors, shapes and light, the newly sighted person's world is vastly different. Their old world, or the context of being blind and not able to see has been transformed. Their new world is filled with light, color, shapes, and movement. They've stepped into a whole new context.

When we stay within the same context, doing what we've always done, we experience frustration. How is it that we expect different results, yet take the same actions? When things aren't working or we want a breakthrough, the most powerful step to take is to consciously change the context, not the content.

"If we keep doing what we've always done, we keep getting what we've always gotten".
~ Tony Robbins

The following is a great example:

~ Gabrielle, age 60, married for 30 years

"When my daughters left home I found myself alone with my husband. My narrative, or the context in which I'd been living, was as wife and mother. The change was bewildering at first, and I sought help. A therapist and the women in my women's group assisted me in identifying the skill sets I cultivated as a mother, as well as creating a new narrative.

One of the most transformational contextual shifts we've undergone has been that of making our family home into a community home. As a couple and homeowners, it's been quite the research project sharing our space with new people. We're learning to be flexible around others' needs, and letting go of attachments that no longer serve us.

My things used to feel like my identity. Now I'm ready to give up my formal living room furniture, though my husband doesn't agree... yet! The issues we now deal with are very different from the ones in the past. We are learning what it's like to live with others, to make consensual decisions, to use deliberate communication skill sets in our house meetings. It's a trip! And we are having more fun than ever!"

Dealing at a contextual level allows for more effectiveness and creativity. Our ability to see where we've been on the basis of context, makes it possible for old ways of being and doing to stop defining who we are. It's not that we escape them—rather that we're able to recognize when we are thinking reflexively. It's in the recognition that the new possibility becomes clear.

Once we've made the distinction between how we see things and who we are, what we see is a result of who we are. Nothing is more exciting than to see the world in a new way because we don't see one new thing—we see everything in a new way. The previously unimaginable becomes possible.

Sudden contextual shifts can be unnerving and shocking, especially if we didn't cause them. When I was just 27, my mother (age 52) was diagnosed with terminal colon cancer. I remember exactly where I was sitting when my father called with the news that her cancer had spread. My brain flooded with questions: 'Mom's sick, oh no... what about Dad, what do I do living 3000 miles away? Will she suffer?'. After a valiant fight for her life, Mom succumbed to the disease. Although I'd had almost two years to integrate her inevitable death, it was still most shocking. The context of having had an intact family as my foundation no longer existed. Luckily, I was able to take the time to say goodbye, emotionally preparing as much as I could.

Then, at the age of forty-eight it was my turn to hear those three dreaded words, "You have cancer". Disbelief, fear, anger, fortitude and determination were the spectrum of emotions I felt. The context of feeling young and indomitable was shattered. A lumpectomy with clean margins and sentinel node biopsy in the right breast, followed by six and a half weeks of radiation treatment, resulted in my cancer going into remission. However, barely a year and a half after round one, an MRI revealed cancer cells in all four quadrants of the left breast. Again, we'd caught it early. Due to there being no set lump to extract, the wisest treatment choice was a mastectomy. I chose to have double mastectomies rather than to endure future mammograms or MRI's with the accompanying fear these diagnostics trigger. I'm happy to be healthy and cancer free ten years later.

First Course: Palate Cleanser – Complete or Repeat Your Past

"Holding onto anger is like grasping a hot coal with the intent of throwing it at someone else; you're the one who gets burned." ~ allegedly, Buddha

How can we expect to start a new life if we're still living in the old one?

Like a great sommelier distinguishes between wine varietals, you should be aware of the distinction between the words complete and finished. Finished means that something has ended, and just because something has ended doesn't mean it's complete or whole. This can be a barrier to fulfilling your desires. When unaddressed, these unfinished ends can obstruct our ability to move forward.

'Complete' means: fulfilled, whole, everything appreciated and acknowledged.

For example, when a relationship ends due to a break up, death, or any other reason, there can be emotional residue preventing you from moving on. The relationship is clearly 'finished', but not necessarily 'complete'. We need to be "complete" about our past if we desire to create a new life.

All relationships have both positive and negative aspects; it's important for each to be acknowledged. Why risk repeating the same patterns that didn't work for you in the past?

"Two monks were traveling together, an older monk and a younger monk. They noticed a young woman at the edge of a stream, afraid to cross. The older monk picked her up, carried her across the stream and put her down safely on the other side. The younger monk was astonished, but he didn't say anything until their journey was over. "Why did you carry that woman across the stream? Monks aren't supposed to touch any member of the opposite sex." said the younger monk. The older monk replied "I left her at the edge of the river. Why is it that you're still carrying her?" ~ Unknown

The following **Seven Step Completion Process** (created by Bill Lamond) will assist you in coming to completion with your past. It provides a structure to acknowledge and release aspects of past relationships, both pleasurable as well as not, in order to move forward into a new life. It's not possible to truly be present or create a future for yourself if you are stuck in the past.

When you're complete with your past, it's easier to develop a new, irresistible future. This process is a powerful tool that takes time and practice, and can be applied to many areas of your life.

Here are some examples of completions you may wish to do:

- A former partner (recent break up or one from ages ago)
- A teacher or fellow student who was mean to you
- A family member, friend or pet who has died

"The problem is never how to get new, innovative thoughts into your mind, but how to get old ones out. Every mind is a building filled with archaic furniture. Clean out a corner of your mind and creativity will instantly fill it." ~Dee Hock

Seven Step Completion Process

Choose a project, issue or relationship that you want to bring to completion. Think of the word complete as meaning: fulfilled, whole, everything appreciated/acknowledged, all files updated, being current. Make a distinction in your thinking between complete and finished. Finished means that something has ended, and just because something has ended doesn't mean it is complete or whole.

1) What gave you pleasure?
When you have completed a list of everything that has given you pleasure, imagine that you are saving all of these pleasurable memories and feelings associated with them into a long-term inactive memory (like the hard drive on your computer.)

2) What did not give you pleasure? When you have completed this list, imagine deleting all the displeasure, pain or suffering from your memory.

3) Forgiveness: Determine who you need to forgive and for what specifically. When you have finished this list, imagine sending your forgiveness out to be received and then delete this list from your memory.

4) Acknowledgements: Now determine who you need to acknowledge or thank and for what, regarding the subject you are completing. When you have finished this list of everything and everyone that you need to acknowledge, imagine sending your acknowledgements out to be received and then delete this list from your memory.

5) Anything else? Ask yourself if there is anything else you need to say to be complete up to the present moment. If it is something that gave you pleasure, then add it to the list you saved (#2 above). Whatever else came to mind, imagine deleting as you did in #'s 3-5.

6) Declaration of Completion: Now declare this project, issue or relationship, complete up to the present moment.

7) Install a new future Since nature abhors a vacuum, declare a new positive affirmation, thus installing a new future concerning the project, issue or relationship.

If you've done your completion process on a past potentially unhealthy relationship, then your future installation might be something like: "My new relationship with a wonderful, honest man will be completely honorable, pleasurable and irresistible."

Congratulations! You've experienced your first Seven Step Completion Process. Where else might you feel incomplete? While the process is fresh in your mind, make a list of other relationships you may want to complete to facilitate moving forward.

Here are several categories to get you thinking about where you might not be complete:
• Friends or relatives who've passed
• A job or career
• A house you sold and miss—or one that you wish to sell
• Habits or addictions
• Beliefs (such as feeling like you are unworthy)
• Those extra pounds

Relapse is an important, and many times inevitable part of completing our past and moving on. If done thoroughly, the Completion Process is comprehensive. Yet the more significant a relationship, the more habits have been woven into your lifestyle - which means the more habits you have to change! The saying "Old habits die hard" applies here.

Remember: When babies fall as they learn to walk, they get back up. They don't say, "I'm stupid...."

We need to be kind to ourselves! Changes take time, and releasing emotions that are stubbornly clinging to us is necessary to move forward. I invite you to be gentle with yourself and take time to integrate.

Releasing Emotions

"Unexpressed emotions will never die. They are buried alive and will come forth later in uglier ways."
~Sigmund Freud

Emotions aren't right or wrong. It's the reactions to feelings that can be judged right or wrong. When you suppress emotions, they get buried in your subconscious. It's no fun to be triggered by a situation when you're least expecting it.

Just a few months after my Mom passed away I was at a crowded movie theatre. The film included several scenes in a hospital waiting room where the same patients came for chemotherapy appointments week after week. One of the patients, a sweet older woman, knitted the same yellow sweater every time she went in for a treatment. One day there was an empty chair with just the ball of yellow yarn, kitting needles and half finished sweater.

Reminding me of my mom and the sweater she'd never completed, I was utterly overwhelmed by the bowling ball of emotions that slammed into my heart. Sobbing, I crawled over dozens of people to get to the exit door.

I cried for days and found a therapist who helped me work through my grief in a healthy manner. I also joined a grief support group which was very helpful.

When a loved one dies there are an inevitable amount of details, as well as many family and friends around all the time. In other words, there is plenty to keep us busy and distracted from stopping long enough to feel. Though I'd certainly had my share of tears during mom's illness, I hadn't allowed myself to drop into the depth of emotions necessary to release the grief.

Two days after she buried her husband, Pat spent three weeks at a retreat doing a deep mind, body and spiritual cleanse surrounded by like-minded people. Afterwards, she felt cleaned out on every level and ready to start her new life. Shortly thereafter she met a wonderful man who's now stepdad to her children.

The end of any intimate relationship needs to be treated as a death of sorts.

As when a loved one dies, there can be a lot of tasks that distract us from taking the time we need to get in touch with our feelings. Please allow yourself the space to create whatever you need to move through and beyond this chapter in your life.

Recipe for Releasing Emotions

- ▶ Live in the present – breathe!
- ▶ Be aware of and take care of your body
- ▶ Give yourself a retreat
- ▶ Exercise
- ▶ Dance
- ▶ Laugh lots
- ▶ Journal about your feelings or write a letter
- ▶ Appreciate the people in your life
- ▶ Meditate
- ▶ Listen to or make your own music
- ▶ Yoga
- ▶ Jump up and down, put your head into a pillow and scream, shaking your whole body at the same time. Let it out!
- ▶ Call your girlfriends!

Second Course - Create Your Irresistible Life: What's on the Menu?

If you've gone through The Completion Process, then you are clear about what has and hasn't given you pleasure in your past relationships. Now's the time to take your enjoyable memories with you and leave the rest behind! You are free to embark on the exciting 'culinary' journey of creating your irresistible life!

As you prepare to clarify your criteria for calling in what you desire, let's bring attention to a few distinctions, starting with some definitions.

Distinction between Hunger and Appetite

First, let's make the distinction between "being hungry" and "having an appetite".

Hunger is survival based, whereas appetite is generated from your desire. We've all seen images of starving, malnourished children. They have distended bellies, and skinny arms and legs. If you were to offer a plate of food to a truly starving child, chances are they wouldn't have enough energy to eat. Or, if they weren't completely starving, they might gobble the entire amount and not be able to keep it down. A few drops of water and perhaps one grain of rice at a time allows for slowly but surely restoring health and wellbeing. The same spectrum applies for any starving creature, regardless of sex or species.

If you were truly hungry, you would be living your life hand to mouth, worrying about your next meal. There could be areas of your life in which you feel a deficit, likened to hunger. For example, you might have enough food, but you wish you had more friends. Maybe you're working so hard that you've forgotten that the beach is less than a mile away.

Now, let's talk about appetite.

Having an appetite is not the same as being hungry. Nor is it about having a goal or an intention. Goals can come out of your commitment to having your appetite fulfilled. Actions are generated from your commitment and goals.

For example, you've been living alone since your marriage ended. You work hard at a job you like, make more than enough money, live in a nice home, have plenty to eat and have a lovely wardrobe. Yet you go to bed alone; you wake up alone. You long to be held, to cuddle and make love. You are experiencing some hunger with respect to intimacy.

People who generate their lives from their appetite rather than from hunger, have the privilege to choose freely – simply for the pleasure of it.

Here's a new spin on other familiar, yet, underused words:

Irresistible:
1. Impossible to resist.
2. Having an overpowering appeal.

Unreasonable:
1. Not governed by or predicated upon reason.
2. Exceeding reasonable limits; exorbitant; immoderate.

"The reasonable man adapts himself to the world; the unreasonable one persists in trying to adapt the world to himself. Therefore, all progress depends on the unreasonable man." ~George Bernard Shaw

- What is your appetite and where might you experience hunger?
- What do you find irresistible?
- What gives you pleasure?
- How unreasonable are you willing to be to create your irresistible life?

"Pleasure is nature's test, her sign of approval. When man is happy, he is in harmony with himself and his environment." ~ Oscar Wilde

Sink down into your place of deep desire. Tap into a younger version of yourself who still believed she could have or be anything she desired! The first thing that comes to mind, no matter how far out of reach it may seem, usually represents a true desire. Go for it without censoring yourself!

"When you pay attention to your pleasure your desires start growing inside and outside of you like hundreds of tiny green shoots sprouting upwards to the glory of the sky above." ~ Regena Thomashauer aka Mama Gena

Pleasure, desire, appetite and irresistibility are subjective. When you're looking at what you'd like to create for yourself, start by going for what's irresistible!

Some Questions to Whet Your Appetite :

Family and Friends

- Are you spending enough time with your children?
- Do you wish you could visit your elderly parents more often?
- Are you having fun with girlfriends?
- Are you dating?
- Do you need support with your online dating profiles?
- Are you cuddling enough?
- Do you want to have (or adopt) a baby?

Your Home Environment:

- Are you surrounded by things that make you feel good?
- Are you living where you wish to live?
- If you're lonely, have you considered living with others?
- Have you considered getting a puppy or a kitten?
- Would you like to have a vegetable or flower garden?

Work and Your Creative Expression:

- Could it be time to quit the job you've hated?
- Is this a good time to start the business you've dreamed about for years?
- How about taking the painting class you've secretly coveted?
- What about volunteering as a docent for the local museum of art?
- Perhaps it would feel great to redecorate your home?

Vacations, Travel and Adventure:

- Do you have a bucket list for places you'd like to go and at least one trip on your calendar?

- The world is a big place! Here's a quick list of possibilities to get your taste buds attuned:
- Trekking in Bhutan
- Scuba diving at the Great Barrier Reef
- Kayaking in Alaska
- Touring the White House
- A river cruise somewhere in Europe
- An African Safari
- A bicycle trip through Tuscany's wine country

Your Spirituality:

- Is it time for you to take that meditation retreat you've talked about for years?
- Do you want to start going to church again?
- Ready to study shamanism or Astrology?
- Would you like to start up a yoga practice?

Your Body

- Have you been thinking about getting into shape?
- Might it be time to do a deep physical cleanse?
- Are you getting enough sleep?
- How about curling up with your cat for a nap?
- Does horseback riding sound fun?
- Would you like to run a marathon?

Third Course - Delicious Beginnings through Deliberate Communication

"Communication leads to community, that is, to understanding, intimacy and mutual valuing."
~Rollo May

Once you're clear about what's irresistible to you, it's time to let others know.

Clients consistently report that communication breakdowns with their significant others are the primary source for subsequent break-ups. Focusing on the negative, or what isn't working, can blind us to the positive that the relationship was built upon to begin with! Complaints pile up and next thing we know the negative has usurped the positive and our relationship implodes.

Deliberate and Responsible Communication

"Communication is a skill that you can learn. It's like riding a bicycle or typing. If you're willing to work at it, you can rapidly improve the quality of every part of your life." ~ Brian Tracy

There are no shortage of communication courses being taught in both traditional academic as well as personal development arenas. An example of one well-known style is Non-Violent Communication (NVC) which was developed by Marshall Rosenberg.

"When our communication supports compassionate giving and receiving, happiness replaces violence and grieving!"
~ CNVC(Center for Non-Violent Communication) founder, Marshall B. Rosenberg, PhD

Marshall told a story of NVC even being used effectively to assist in negotiations between Israeli and Palestinians civilians. Though NVC is an excellent and highly respectable practice, in order for it to work effectively, much study and active participation is required by all parties. Something as comprehensive and intricate as NVC is not necessary when you simply need some tools to assist you in being kind and direct with your partner.

During three decades of research in personal development, I've been exposed to and studied many additional effective communication modalities. The following three offered below have been adapted from practices created and utilized by an ongoing intentional community based in the San Francisco Bay Area called Morehouse. Originally created by its founder Victor Baranko, these communication tools are simple to learn and extremely effective. They can be used in both your professional and personal life. And, like anything new, practice is required in order to attain at least enough mastery to use them effectively.

The three communication modalities are:

1. A.R.T.Full™ communication (Appreciate, Request, Thank)
2. Appreciation Process
3. Withhold Process

A.R.T. Full Communication

We had a wonderful dinner party with friends. I'd spent much of the day cooking and preparing for our evening, and after great food and conversation, our friends left. My husband Billy and I had a deal. When I cooked, he did the dishes.

The clanging and banging went on, as I'd left him quite a mess. After awhile I went down to check on his progress, and I'd been looking forward to cuddling.

When I walked into the kitchen I noticed that the dishwasher was running, the pots and pans were neatly stacked and crumbs were all... over the counters. Billy was setting down a dishtowel and his hand was reaching to turn off the light. He was clearly finished, ready to head upstairs.

Imagine a TV game show in terms of the choices one can make... door #1, 2, and 3. Clearly there's a best choice, a lesser choice and usually a poor choice.

Here's how our conversation went:

'Door Number One' scenario

Me:
"Will you please wipe the counters before you come upstairs?"

Billy:
"You didn't even notice how much I've done? - You teach this communication stuff!"

He then stormed out of the room and went to watch TV. After that, he refused to speak with me, and slept in the guest room. So much for the sexy date I'd been anticipating.

You know what? His response was absolutely justified! Rather than acknowledging him for his good work, I'd pointed out what he hadn't done.

Thus, Door Number One was clearly not a good choice!

Again, same situation, two different possible outcomes:

'Door Number Two' scenario

Me:
A (Appreciate) – "Wow, awesome job cleaning up the epic mess I made."

R (Request) – "Would you mind wiping the counters before you come upstairs?"

T (Thank) – "Thanks!"

Me:
"Awesome job, Babe. See you upstairs! And then I'd wipe the counters myself and join him upstairs for our anticipated intimate connection."

"Sure."
or
"Would you mind wiping the counters yourself? I'm exhausted and will see you upstairs."

Either way, no one was acting defensive or angry and that sexy date would have happened after all!

'Door Number Three' scenario
(probably the best choice!)

The above example really happened! From bedroom to boardroom, I invite you to practice this technique. Like anything, practice leads to mastery!

Recipe for A.R.T. Full Communication:

A (Appreciate) – Find something (anything!) you like and express that

R (Request) – Make a small request (best if it can garner a yes or no response)

T (Thank) – Thank them even if they haven't fulfilled your request yet! (In other words, they still need more guidance!)

Repeat the process until you're satisfied!

"Wow! I can't believe how effective the A.R.T.-full technique was with my fiancé! Having raised three of my own children with clear boundaries regarding bedtime, etc., I was uncomfortable with how 'loose' his boundaries were with his ten year old daughter who lives with us half time. The lack of a clear bedtime was cutting into our intimate time, and I found myself getting annoyed. A.R.T. gave me the perfect way to communicate clearly and kindly with him, and it worked! His daughter now knows exactly when bedtime is and we have more time together."
~ Marcia, age 45, financial planner

This translates to everywhere in our lives... from the bedroom to the boardroom. I invite you to practice using this technique in the kitchen or at the office prior to trying it out when making love to your partner. Like anything, practice leads to mastery!

Here are other examples where A.R.T.Full can make a tremendous difference:

Example: Your employee or student has handed in sub par work.

How NOT to respond:

"That's not what I was looking for. I expect something better."

Here's a better way to respond using this model:

A- "What a great first draft."
R- "Will you please do another rendition with more attention to detail?
T- "Thanks!"

Example: You don't like the way your lover is touching you, as it tickles.

How NOT to respond: "I've told you I hate being tickled."

How to respond using A.R.T.Full:

A - I love that you want me to feel good.

R - Will you please touch me a little harder?

T - Thanks!

More examples of when to use A.R.T Full.:

• When potty training your child

• When communicating to your housekeeper (or anyone!) you'd like something done differently

- Letting your roommate (or teenager!) know you'd like them to complete a chore they neglected

Can you think of other times and places in your life where you might use this specific form of communication?

"A great relationship has great communication. That means knowing how to effectively express yourself and how to listen properly." ~ Stephan Labossiere

The Appreciation Process

"Appreciation can make a day, even change a life. Your willingness to put it into words is all that is necessary." ~ Margaret Cousins

It's common knowledge that children thrive on being appreciated. Rewards such as M & M's, gold stars and verbal praise can go a long way when you're teaching new behaviors from potty training to turning homework assignments in on time.

Birthdays, Christmas, Valentine's Day all provide gift-giving opportunities. We use flowers, chocolates, trophies and medals to let someone know we love them, and acknowledge their accomplishments. Yet when it comes to letting our most intimate partners  know we appreciate them, we tend to fall short. Especially after we've been together for awhile, we take for granted the little things. For most of us, having the same partner for eons typically does not spark the kind of sexual excitement experienced when the relationship was new. But this isn't an excuse to stop expressing your appreciation!

When we give a gift, including verbal appreciation it usually results in our liking that person more. It's like making an investment in them. Good investments grow.

Andrea and Ted

Andrea participated in my Men, Sex & Money® seminar. Not only did she leave the seminar with a sense of how important self care was after years of putting her time and attention into raising her son, she also realized how the relationship with her boyfriend was not meeting her needs. She'd been "ordering short", and was no longer willing to settle!

She loved Ted for his intellect and how much they laughed together. They had lots in common, and she adored his kids with whom she'd become bonded. But this wasn't enough! She wanted to feel beautiful and sexy. He never let her know he appreciated her, rarely complimented her and would only make love occasionally and with reluctance. Andrea felt lonely and sexually frustrated.

Feeling hopeless, she asked if I'd help them break up in a mature and civil way. I'll never forget their first session. She sat on one section of my couch, there was an empty section between them and he sat on another section. Their body language was stiff as they sat turned away from one another. I sat facing Andrea, suggesting she stay focused on me. I asked Ted to simply watch us from his vantage place a few feet away.

I set a timer for three minutes, and used the Appreciation Process as follows:

Me: Andrea, tell me something you appreciate about Ted.

Andrea: I appreciate that he makes me dinner on the nights I work late.

Me: Thank you.

Me: Andrea, tell me something you appreciate about Ted.

Andrea: I love the way he's parenting his kids.

Me: Thank you.

Me: Andrea, tell me something you appreciate about Ted

Andrea: I like going on camping trips with him

Me: Thank you.

I repeated the same cycle for three minutes. When the timer went off I was stunned to see tears running down Ted's cheeks. He told us he had no idea Andrea appreciated him at all! They'd simply spent so much time focused on what wasn't working, they'd forgotten what brought them together in the first place!

I then repeated the same three minute cycle asking Ted what he appreciated about Andrea. This time it was Andrea's turn to be in tears. Slowly but surely their bodies were relaxing and they started to lean in toward one another.

I did one more round of "Appreciations" each, for a TOTAL of twelve minutes. Though I've used this process for decades, I was astonished at its effectiveness in such a short amount of time!

"Appreciation is a wonderful thing. It makes what is excellent in others belong to us as well." ~Voltaire

Recipe for The Appreciation Process

Person A : "There's something I'd like to appreciate about you."

Person B : "Okay, would you like to tell me?"

Person A : "It was wonderful to come home to find dinner on the table!"

Person B : "Thank you." (spoken neutrally no matter what feelings have been evoked. This keeps it "safe" for true feelings to be expressed.

The Withhold Process: A Great Way to Clear the Air

"Some people will not tolerate such emotional honesty in communication. They would rather defend their dishonesty on the grounds that it might hurt others. Therefore, having rationalized their phoniness into nobility, they settle for superficial relationships." ~Author Unknown

Let's face it. Most people are afraid to tell the truth if they think it might hurt someone's feelings. So they withhold less than pleasant communication rather than express it in the moment. This can lead to a build up of issues resulting in some sort of breakdown or altercation that didn't need to occur if addressed along the way. Ever hear of a couple breaking up over some seemingly petty issue? Most likely that one issue we heard about was simply the "last straw" in a long line of minor transgressions that were not confronted earlier. So rather than allow a build up of negative energy, The Withhold Process offers an easy and streamlined solution that makes it safe to communicate and thus clear the air between you and others. This opens the way to more love!

"Truth is the most valuable thing we have. Let us economize it." ~Mark Twain

Isn't it kinder to tell someone that their fly is down or that they have kale stuck in their teeth before they embarrass themselves in public? I know I feel respected when someone tells me something similar! It's a terrible feeling to get home from an event and realize you've spent the past several hours with green stuff stuck in your teeth and no one had the decency to tell you. What about letting your lover know that you'd prefer not to kiss them because they have bad breath; or body odor?

While A.R.T.Full Communication can go a long way helping to make requests, sometimes, particularly in our most intimate relationships, small issues can build up until we notice we're ready to bail rather than confront the truth!

Rather than hold onto thoughts that are bothering you, The Withhold Process offers a great solution.

Withholds refer to anything we haven't communicated to another person. They are un-communicated charge, or energy – both positive and negative that exist between us. An example of a positive charge might be that you've neglected to tell your friend how much you appreciated the favor they did for you. A negative charge could include letting them know how frustrated you were when they arrived late, making both of you miss the beginning of a show.

What have you withheld - or not said - to your partner? Harboring secrets or communication that might be challenging from the people closest to you can create a fissure. This can fester into something that becomes too large to dispel, and the relationship might not survive. The term "There's an elephant in the living room" sums up the concept.

*"Elephant in the living room is an English idiom for an obvious truth that is going unaddressed. The idiomatic expression also applies to an obvious problem or risk no one wants to discuss.
It is based on the idea that an elephant in a room would be impossible to overlook." ~Wikipedia*

What might need to be said so that you can feel the love between you again?

This is a good question to ask each other during times of tension. If you already have an effective communication method that allows you to easily and directly inform one another—particularly about the tough subjects—with neither of you becoming defensive or blaming the other, then keep doing what you've been doing. However if you're like most, it's not so easy to be direct-especially about the tougher subjects. In other words, you have a criticism or complaint, and no matter how valid, it may not be easy to convey this in a kind yet constructive manner. It might be even more difficult for the recipient to receive the communication without reacting defensively.

Two Recipes for Delivering Withholds

PULLING WITHHOLDS:

Person A: Tell me something you've withheld from me.

Person B: It hurt my feelings when you were late to dinner.

Person A: Thank you. (Spoken neutrally, keeping it "safe" for the person to express their truth.)

GENERATING WITHHOLDS:

Person A: There's something I've withheld from you.

Person B: OK, would you like to tell me.

(Keep a neutral expression)

Person A: It really pissed me off that you were late to the meeting yesterday.

Person B: Thank you. (Again, keep a neutral face)

Note the following:

1. While delivering a withhold, the person communicating is free to express any and all emotions.

2. The person receiving a withhold must remain completely neutral to create safety for the person communicating.

3. The content of withholds does not get discussed at a later point in time unless a clear agreement exists between the two people. Again, this creates the safe container into which people can express themselves.

4. When an extremely high charge exists between two people, we recommend that a third, neutral party be present for this process.

When consciously and appropriately delivered, the Withhold Process results in reducing the charge, making it possible for a much greater level of affinity and love to exist. Withholds are a way for us to be responsible for our own charge, while creating more freedom with the people we care about. This tool is also a powerful way to empty our minds so that we can be more present.

What happened with Andrea and Ted?

After building the foundation of appreciation that they'd covered over with built up anger and resentments, we did several rounds of withholds. This tool created the structure to let each another know about unexpressed issues, all without either of them falling into the game of shame, blame, and victimhood.

They left with the homework to give one another a minimum of three appreciations upon waking each morning. They were instructed to repeat this before going to bed. No appreciation is too small, and you can never give too many!

They showed up for their second session holdings hands while they sat next to one another. By the third session they informed me they'd found a house to move into together. Two years later, they announced their engagement!

Can you think of things you've hesitated to say to the people closest to you, both positive as well as not so positive?

I encourage you to give these processes a chance, though at first they may seem awkward. Kids love them, as they make it easy to express their truth in a safe, clean and clear way. The carefully structured wording makes it easy for even quiet and shy people to have equal access to express themselves.

Fourth Course - Family Style: Reach for Connection

Connection is the energy that is created between people when they feel seen heard and valued—when they can give and receive without judgment."
~Brene Brown, PhD, LMSW

We all need to love and be loved – both sexually and non-sexually. Loneliness, social anxiety, and even clinical depression can occur without it. The need to love and belong includes the need for relationships, social connections, the need to give and receive affection, as well as to feel part of a group.

Abraham Maslow's Hierarchy of Needs represents a popular framework in psychology. It's based on the premise that once individual physiological and safety needs are met, the next level of human needs is to feel a sense of acceptance among social groups. Larger groups include clubs, fellow students, co-workers, religious groups, professional organizations, sports teams or even gangs.

Smaller social connections include family members, intimate partners, women's groups, mentors, colleagues, and confidantes.

"A community is made up of intimate relationships among diversified types of individuals - a kinship group, a local group, a neighborhood, a village, a large family." ~Carroll Quigley

If you're considering relocating, think about who you know or what organization might help you get connected. People like to help people, so don't be afraid to ask for support. Now's not the time to be shy!

"A city is a large community where people are lonesome together." ~Herbert Prochnow

How to Create Meaningful Connections

"The hardest part about starting over has been how disenfranchised I've felt since arriving in Southern California. My move was inspired by my need to part ways from my partner, as I simply couldn't deal with being in close proximity, as it was too tempting to fall back into our intimacy, though we both knew it was no longer serving us. So my friends are all back in Hawaii where I lived for almost a decade, and my family is in Northern California. Now that I've become part of a women's group that meets regularly, I'm beginning to feel more at home here. I've got my girlfriends and they've got my back!" ~ Mary, age 63

"A few months after my divorce was final I jumped into volunteering with a not for profit. Making a difference for a common cause connected me with like minded people, and gave me the sense of belonging I'd been missing." ~ Susie, age 58

When my husband and I separated I was faced with the daunting task of reinventing myself. As a homeowner living a semi-retired lifestyle, I'd been focused on leading my seminars for young women, hosting fundraisers for my favorite not for profit organizations, enjoying travels to exotic places and was accustomed to social circles comprised primarily of couples. We celebrated the holidays, traveled and basically lived our lives with mutual friends, most of whom were married. Overcome by the myriad details of selling my home and separating, I wasn't prepared for how all those dynamics would change when Billy and I decided to go our separate ways. Suddenly, the familiar aspects of my identity no longer provided me my foundation. I had no idea what to do, where to go, never mind how to relate on my own in the world.

Even though we mutually chose to leave our marriage and were parting as friends, the changes were traumatizing. My home, husband, community, the lifestyle to which I'd been accustomed for fifteen years—all gone.

In addition to my therapist and women's group, I am grateful to have had friends who loved me, patiently listened, and held me through my grief and helped me start over one day at a time. Yet nothing prepared me for just how disoriented and confused I became. Fortunately, I found it easy to connect with people, which is not the case for everyone starting over.

"Strangers are just friends you haven't met yet!"

My mother used to tell a funny story about me as a fourteen month old. Dad was a flight surgeon in the Air Force, and we were on a plane en route home to the United States from France, where we'd lived in a trailer on an Air Force base since I'd been born. An elderly Frenchman was sitting behind us. I leaned over the seat, grabbed his rather substantial nose and exclaimed, "Hi man!" Mom said he threw back his head and laughed. She also said I never changed; that I have always been prone to meet and befriend strangers, and she was right!

I am grateful for this natural ability to connect with strangers, as I do see most people as potential friends. Yet I know not everyone is inherently outgoing, but may be introverted and shy. It could be that even making eye contact with someone you don't know makes you feel uncomfortable.

The fear of strangers might certainly be a direct result of the "don't talk to strangers" warnings many of us received as children. If you, like me, were brought up in the 1960's, when the world was a safer place, it was even considered well mannered and kind to befriend someone new.

"Taking the time to build community, to get to know your people, will have long lasting benefits."
~Clifton Taulbert

Looking back, one thing that most helped create a sense of belonging in our West Sonoma County community, was participating in a women's group known as the Wild Darlin's. When Billy and I moved to Sonoma County, we knew only a few people. I was very fortunate that Suzie, a friend I'd known for years, invited me to join a monthly women's group. Now in its 17th year, the Darlin's have been meeting over dinner on the first Tuesday of every month since. We've seen one another through marriages, divorces, glorified in the accomplishments of children as well as supported one another though the tough times. We've taken vacations in Mexico, and have even supported one of our beloved members through her diagnosis and subsequent death from cancer. Though I've moved 650 miles south, I stay connected with these amazing Darlin's when I can get myself to the Bay Area. The group, though I can rarely attend, still serves as a grounding cord. I'm pleased to have created a women's group here in San Diego County. We meet twice a month and are each grateful for the mutual friendship and support. Girlfriends make all the difference, especially in a place where one has no family!

"There is a community of the spirit. Join it and feel the delight of walking in the noisy street and being the noise." ~Rumi

Recipe to Create Your Support Network

- Make a list of everything you like to do, and find ways to do them!

- Connect with a stranger and cultivate a new friendship.

- Volunteer! Nothing feels better than making a difference. Do so with an organization you respect as you'll have more in common with other volunteers.

- Check out MeetUp.com. Search under subjects of interest to you. MeetUps vastly range from business networking meetings to singles who go to comedy clubs, to Chihuahua owners, to tantra sexuality groups.

- Start your own MeetUp (it's easy to do). One woman who just moved and felt lonely started a MeetUp called "Family Dinners for People without Family". She clearly hit a chord of need, given that within the first twenty four hours since she posted it, over fifty people had joined the group!

- Invite acquaintances out to coffee or lunch.

- Throw a party.

- Join Facebook groups and remember to regularly check your notification and invite lists on FB.

- On-lining dating can garner new friends as well as a potential intimate relationship.

- Attend conferences and festivals about things that atter to you; a great way to meet like-minded people!

- Offer your services to a friend in need.

- ▶ Hire an assistant.

- ▶ Reach out to friends or family rather than isolate! A FaceTime or Skype phone call can be helpful when you're feeling lonely.

- ▶ If you're an entrepreneur, rather than working at home by yourself, consider renting space in a cooperative office environment.

- ▶ Get a puppy or dog and go to the dog parks. This is a great way to connect with others, not to mention having a furry friend for yourself.

- ▶ Make yourself go out even if not feeling inclined; there are coffee shops on every corner.

- ▶ Go shopping and have a chat with a sales person or fellow shopper.

- ▶ Play a sport. There are MeetUps for every sport imaginable!

- ▶ Join a support group for women, or for men (MeetUp has a wide variety).

- ▶ Start a support group for yourself. This could be a book group, knitting circle, wine or beer tasting or whatever else appeals to you.

- ▶ Lastly, give yourself space to make new contacts.

Recipe for Turning Strangers into Friends

Smile ~ as you make eye contact with someone, a smile makes them and you feel more comfortable and will most likely be reciprocated.

Observe ~ something you might have in common and comment. The possibilities are endless! It could be a compliment on their clothing choice or if you're feeling frisky, on their lovely blue eyes, the weather, a current event, laughing about their or your puppy's antics... there's no shortage of conversation!

Be interested ~ Ask a question and LISTEN to their answer. Though it's tempting to immediately relate their story to yours, be conscious about not "stealing the story" from them. Remember, you asked!

Fifth Course – Dealing with Your Kitchen Makeover

No Body = Nobody!
By now you recognize the importance of doing the inner work of releasing what no longer serves us in order to start over.
- How do you feel?
- Are you in excellent health? If not, what will it take?
- Are you nourishing your body with healthy food and supplementation?
- Are you exercising?
- When was your last medical checkup?
- Do you sleep enough?
- Do you treat yourself to massages and/or facials?
- How sexy and vibrant do you feel?
- Do you avoid the scale or feel fine about your weight?

Menopause
Who me? No libido? No way!
I'd heard stories from friends about their extreme menopause related symptoms. Tears, bouts of unprovoked anger, hot flashes, nausea, headaches, mood swings, depression, even personality changes all sounded terrible. Reports about women's libido falling flat, vaginal dryness and discomfort during intercourse made the prospect all the more daunting. Instead, at the age of 53 (after 39 years of a 28-30 day cycle) my period abruptly ended. Married at the time, I was grateful to have sailed through menopause 'seemingly unscathed'.

A healthy libido and satisfying sex life had been an integral part of my life. I never imagined that life might some day be different.

Since my journey through menopause had been uneventful, it was shocking to find myself unable to have intercourse. Though older women friends had spoken about their discomfort with penetration post menopause, I never thought that I'd experience burning pain of 10 on a scale of 1-5!

The cause of vaginal atrophy is usually the normal decrease in estrogen as a result of menopause. Other causes of decreased estrogen levels are decreased ovarian functioning due to radiation therapy or chemotherapy, immune disorder, removal of the ovaries, entering the post-partum period, and lactation.

Horrified and unwilling to live the rest of my life feeling dried up, I did research resulting in the choice to do hormone therapy.

"In peri-menopause our brains are being rewired to live with more inner wisdom, to adapt to a more direct current (intuition); and we may experience insomnia, forgetfulness and depression. It takes a great deal of courage and faith to go through this change, and some women go through painful breakdowns before they are ready to relinquish the struggle for control." ~Dr. Christiane Northrup, The Wisdom of Menopause

Different approaches to hormone supplementation range from products you can get at a health food store such as creams and tablets, to prescription bio-identical creams created by compounding pharmacies.

I consulted a specialist, and within six weeks, the energetic and juicy woman I'd always known returned. Sex was not only no longer painful, it was more pleasurable than it had been. Now, rather than cringe when asked my age, I delight in people's astonishment when I tell them.

"Menopause is thicker than water. When we talk and laugh about it, we learn and relax. It's a life transition, not a disease." ~ Anonymous

There's More than one Lifestyle Choice

Bonnie, age 63

"Since going through menopause in my early 50's, this last decade has been wonderful. I sold the home where I raised my family in the city and bought a house overlooking the water in West Marin County. I have a sweet little dog and much of my time and attention is focused on my grandchildren. This has enabled my daughter to start her dream business. And, although I always had a wonderful sex life, I don't miss it and am content."

After her marriage ended and she went through menopause, she felt no desire to be in another sexual relationship. This lifestyle choice worked for Bonnie.

Challenges come when one partner still feels frisky, while the other would rather be reading a good book.

If you're post-menopausal and find yourself with no libido, challenges occur if your partner is still filled with sexual desire.

Men Have Cycles Too! Though considerably different physiologically, some men experience their version of a change of life known as Andropause. This sometimes results in the classic "midlife crisis".

A gradual decline in the production of the androgenic hormones (testosterone) can result in a variety of symptoms. These can include depression, loss of libido, erectile dysfunction, as well as irritability, loss of muscle mass and reduced ability to exercise, weight gain and a lack of energy. We've all heard of men having a midlife crisis during which they buy a sports car, a motorcycle or have an affair with a younger woman. I smile remembering my prior husband buying a motorcycle for his 50th, followed by an RV for his 60th!

Plastic Surgery as an Option

What's the first thing you see when you look at yourself in the mirror?

- Shiny hair?
- Beautiful smile?
- Sparkly eyes?
- Smooth skin?
- Gorgeous curves?
- A vital sexy woman?

Or, are you only able to see?

- Drooping eyelids?
- Large breasts hanging to your navel?
- Eyebrow hairs sprouting on your chin?
- Yellow teeth?

In other words, is a dumpy, middle-aged woman staring back at you?

While eating a healthy diet, keeping your weight down, updating your wardrobe, getting a terrific new hairstyle and simply being in your pleasure all positively effect the way others see you, some of the effects of aging simply require a more radical solution.

Plastic Surgery to the Rescue!

I'll never forget lying on the operating room table about to be put under when my plastic surgeon asked, "What size did you say you wanted?"

As a 5'6" woman with a medium frame, I'd always thought I'd look more in proportion if my natural size B breasts were larger. Certainly a mastectomy is not as a way to have the breast augmentation you always wanted. That said, I consider my C cup breast implants to be a silver lining in my whole experience with breast cancer. Despite the lack of sensation I love my new breasts (and the fact I have less than a 2% chance of getting breast cancer again!) I feel that clothing looks better on me and can hardly remember what I looked like before my surgery. As mentioned in the previous chapter, the eye is drawn to imbalances. We notice people and attributes that stand out. Think about it... when you picture Jimmy Durante, you think of his impressive nose. Dolly Parton's chest in contrast to her tiny waist is iconic. Though there are people who believe in aging "naturally", more and more are choosing cosmetic and reconstruction surgeries as well as fillers such as Botox.

"Cosmetic surgery is becoming increasingly popular in America. Some of the plastic surgery procedures that registered growth in the US in 2013 include liposuction (16.3%), eyelid surgery (5.4%), breast augmentation (5.2%), nose surgery (2.9%), and tummy tuck (2.3%). Cosmetic procedures experienced a 12% growth in 2013 alone, with patients spending a staggering $12+ billion over this time period."
~ American Society for Aesthetic Plastic Surgery (ASAPS)

As a kid, looking different than one's peers is a set up for being teased, bullied, isolated and alone. This was particularly true for me, as starting in my early teens my nose grew. Though not huge, it definitely had a prominent bump. It was painful when one of the popular football players at my high school asked me where I got the beak. Ouch. Of course this led me to be self-conscious.

Yet, the size of my nose continued to plague me for the next decade. Simply stated, it stood in the way of my feeling beautiful and normal. Years later, I wrote a New Year's goal to have the nose I'd always desired. Soon after, I walked into a sliding glass door. You guessed it! Medical insurance came to the rescue. The moment the surgeon removed the bandage, the issue I'd suffered with for more than half my life was gone. At last I felt normal; no longer like a misfit.

A beautiful woman friend of mine dated a man whose teeth were unsightly. She made the bold request for him to invest in veneers prior to moving in with her. Understandably, at first he was hurt and hesitant. However, she was clearly irresistible enough such that he went for the deal. After spending the $10,000 required to transform his smile from one who looked homeless to handsome, he was deeply grateful to her (as were all their friends!).

Robin had always had extremely large breasts. At 5'9" she could carry them well, yet after nursing, they became cumbersome, heavy and actually caused her discomfort in her shoulders from their weight. Additionally, they made her look about 20 pounds larger than she was. Breast reduction surgery resulted in her feeling far more comfortable and well proportioned. She was relieved.

Money

It's not just your body that might need updating! The money conversation is the extra salt you have to add for you to live your life in honesty and integrity.

Although not always the case, much of the time divorces are more challenging when financial agreements have not been made clear. While you're dealing with your own potential grief inherent in any separation, if children are in the mix it can get more complicated.

Spending Plans

Many of us tend to be vague when it comes to finances. We are not sure how much money we spend, how much we earn, or simply how much we need to live on a weekly, monthly or yearly basis. Vagueness can wreak havoc in our lives, preventing us from being successful and empowered. Please place your napkin on your lap as I introduce you to the idea of keeping spending records and having concrete spending plans. Note that I'm calling them "spending plans" vs. budgets. The word budget always makes me think there are things I'm not allowed to have, and I immediately become rebellious. However, if it's called a "plan" then that is exactly what it is, giving us control of how we plan, or choose, to spend our money.

It's best to have several spending plans including:

- A "basic spending plan"
- An "ideal spending plan"
- An "over the top spending plan".

A "basic spending plan" is just that: basic. It can include your mortgage or rent, taxes, food, healthcare, car, etc. but not a lot of extras. An "ideal spending plan" includes everything you would consider necessary or required for you to be living your vision of an ideal life. This list might include vacations, a horse, that fancy new car you've been wanting, etc. An "over the top spending plan" could include things like starting your own foundation, having enough money to be able to be philanthropic to your heart's content, a wild adventure to an exotic location, that gorgeous piece of jewelry you've always desired or anything else you might dream up.

When you consider the categories included in your basic spending plan, the key word is basic! Since Individual values differ greatly, what one of you may consider basic may seem like a luxury to another. For instance, health insurance and regular dental cleanings are typically part of a basic spending plan. However, someone might have those items as part of their ideal spending plan. And for someone else, owning and caring for a horse might be on their basic plan, whereas someone else might consider horse ownership to be a luxury.

Wherever you find yourself, it is important to be clear. Vagueness, especially when it comes to money, can be detrimental to your health! And, being vague can wreak havoc in relationships.

A few money concerns:

- Communication around money
- Power struggle over who controls the money
- Sabotage by spending money outside the budget by the one who feels that he/she has no power
- Lack of self-worth around having a low net worth
- Fear of not having enough

The list can go on and on. As you see, money can bring up many different issues. It's not money that's the problem, but how we see ourselves in regards to money. For example, our society was created on the belief that men should be the financial providers, while women stayed home supporting their men. If you've been the breadwinner, inherited money or have a settlement from your divorce, then you may not need a man for financial support, or to be the father of your child. Again, it's all about clarity and communication. The following is a simple worksheet to help you gain more clarity and become more conscious about money.

Personal Basic Spending Plan (example)

1 -Rent/Mortgage

2 -Utilities (water & power, propane, garbage, recycle)

3 -Telephone (basic service, long distance, calling card)

4 -Cell phone

5 -Car: gas, registration, insurance, maintenance including oil changes and major services, parking, bridge tolls

6 -Groceries

7 -Lunches and snacks (while out and about)

8 -Dinners out

9 -Entertainment (movies, etc.)

10 -Household expenses (cleaning products, cleaning service, flowers) homeowners or renter's insurance

11 -Health –necessary prescriptions, aspirin, first aid supplies

-medical insurance, annual physicals including mammogram and other screening

-dental insurance, teeth cleaning, etc.

-eyecare (eyeglasses including accounting for inexpensive reading glasses), - contact lens paraphernalia

-chiropractor or other body work necessary

12 -Well being: gym membership, yoga classes, other exercise classes, massages, lectures

13 -Supplements

14 -Self care: toiletries and cosmetics, haircuts, manicures and pedicures

15 -Gifts, greeting cards

16 -Continuing Ed

17 -Clothing: new, maintenance

18 -Family obligations including travel, vacations

19 -Family expenses i.e. kids clothing, schooling, etc.

20 -Savings

21 -Donations/tithing

22 -Credit card, student loan or other minimum monthly debt payments

23 -Estimated taxes

24 -Pet food and expenses (are you prepared if anything happens to your pet?)

Personal Ideal Spending Plan (example)

Now that you have your Basic Spending Plan, think about what an Ideal Spending Plan might look like. Here are some categories for you to consider adding to your basic spending plan to have your life be more ideal.

1 -Savings

2 -Investments

3 -Major purchases (house, second home, car, furniture, etc.)

4 -House remodel or renovation or simply new décor

5 -Art

6 -Vacations/travel

7 -Retreat

8 -Seminars and workshops

9 -Continuing Ed or degree program

10 -Professional fees i.e. Legal, accountant (will, trusts)

11 -Extra curricular activities such as music or dance lessons

12 -Personal trainer

13 -Enhanced self care i.e. regular facials or massages

14 -Entertainment (more expensive theatre tickets, events)

15 -Wining and dining out

16 -Entertaining at home (with catering, cleaning help)

17 -Housecleaning

18 -Clothing, jewelry, baubles

19 -Skiing, golf or other sport

20 -Gifts (more extravagant)

21 -Xmas gift planning

22 -Cosmetic surgery or dentistry (i.e. Cap that tooth that has troubled you for - years!)

23 -Taxes

24 -Donations (what organizations would you truly like to support and at what level?)

25 -A new pet (horse?)

26 -Music (new audio equipment, a piano, etc)

Here are a few "Over the Top Spending Plan" Ideas:

- Seed money for your foundation
- The sailboat of your dreams
- First class safari in Kenya
- Staying in a penthouse in the city of your choice
- Building your dream house

Sixth Course – Dinner Guests

Dating

You've completed your past relationships. You've allowed yourself to feel and release your emotions. You've attended to your mind, body and spirit and feel great about yourself!

Are you ready to design your next relationship? Here are some helpful distinctions to make it easier.

Expectations and Expectancy

When it comes time to create your wish list regarding a new partner, the following distinction between living with an *expectation* versus living in *expectancy*, might help you. The difference between having a specific *expectation* that something should be, look a certain way can easily lead to disappointment. On the contrary, if you stay in the *expectancy* that it will look and feel better than you can imagine, you might be pleasantly surprised.

Expectation:

You want to meet a partner with the following characteristics:

- Six feet tall
- Weighs 195 pounds
- Has a full head of blonde hair
- Green eyes
- Works as a doctor
- Earns 'X' amount of money

You might be disappointed if your expectations are rigid, as such a specific list makes it challenging to find anyone who meets those exact qualifications.

What if instead, you choose to stay in the Expectancy that the most delightfully attractive and appropriate partner comes into your life?

A way to phrase this might be:

- He's extremely attractive with nice eyes.
- His height and weight are just right for you.
- He has a great career and is financially stable.

Criteria and Preferences

Another way to look at it is to make the distinction between your criteria and preferences.

Your criteria represents your non-negotiables, while your preferences can be negotiated!

When listing the desirable qualities you'd like to find in a potential mate, at one end of the spectrum you list the absolute non-negotiables – in other words, the qualities you absolutely must have. These might include:

- Integrity; a man of his word

- Commitment to excellent health
- Politically liberal or conservative
- A certain religion
- Excellent communication skills
- He plays golf (or doesn't!)
- He's fluent in English
- He's financially responsible
- He's done personal growth

At the opposite end of the spectrum are your deal breakers which could include someone who:

- Drinks or uses drugs
- Doesn't speak English fluently
- Is not financially stable
- Blames others for their mistakes
- Has not cleaned up his last relationship
- Carries lots of extra weight and doesn't take care of their body
- Doesn't have children
- Has never been in a long term committed relationship

Your preferences represent the most desirable traits you seek, yet unlike with your absolute criteria, they are not deal breakers. There's room for negotiation.

It's important to be certain about what you consider an absolute deal breaker.

My friend Robin had always been attracted to tall, thin men with no body hair. Then, when least suspecting, she was swept off her feet by her now husband Steve. In her words, Steve is stocky, exactly her height and furry - hardly the tall, hairless man she'd been seeking! She was humbled to note that what she'd thought was a non-negotiable (criteria) actually had been a preference. She considers Steve the love of her life and they are engaged.

Prior to moving into relationship, it's imperative to know your own intimacy boundaries. First, you need to determine the level of physical/sensual connection that makes you comfortable. Once you are clear, you'll be able to communicate to your new partner what works and what doesn't.

When it comes to your boundaries, "No" is a complete sentence!

Here are several questions to consider moving forward:

- How do I go about meeting a man?
- How do I start a conversation?
- How do I connect with him?
- How do I open my heart again?
- How do I let men know I'm available when, for years, I'd been sending out the signal, 'I am not available'?
- Is it okay at this age and stage to have a friend with benefits as I did in college?
- Do I need to have a safe sex conversation regarding possible pregnancy? What about the risk factors for STD's?
- (It might be decades since you've last been on the dating scene thus you may need to do research about current STD risks and protection considerations) Might you want to have an STD (Sexually Transmitted Disease) test? Is it enough to have him show you his test, or perhaps you want to go to a clinic together?
- Are you okay with a hot kiss on the first date (or would you rather wait)? How sexual are you willing to be?
- When is the time to start talking about exclusivity?
- And if you're not exclusive, what are your agreements?

Each of the above questions represents a much bigger conversation. Please take the time to do as much research required for you to feel comfortable moving forward. The timing of such conversations is important; it's best to be deliberate! It's no fun to be caught up in some wild chemistry and find yourself unprepared.

Who Picks Up the Bill?

Another important aspect of intimacy and relationship is the matter of money. Here I'm referring to all lifestyle choices having to do with finances.

These Include:

- Buying habits
- Vacation styles
- Who pays for what
- Potential prenuptial agreements
- Estate planning
- College funds for children, stepchildren

It doesn't matter if you choose to have separate bedrooms and separate bank accounts. It does matter for you to communicate, particularly about these sensitive issues!

Jason and Rebecca had been dating for several months and things were going well. Rebecca, who was eager to take the relationship to the next level, was thrilled when Jason asked her to go with him to a four-day intimacy workshop. When they arrived, Jason pulled out his checkbook and started to write a check for $595 to cover his tuition. Rebecca, however, made no move to pay. With a sinking feeling, Jason realized Rebecca expected him to pay for her as well. Rather than talking about it, he simply changed the amount of his check to $1190.00. Neither of them said a word.

It won't surprise you to know the workshop wasn't fun for either of them. It doesn't matter who pays, but it does matter if you communicate! This lack of communication ultimately doomed the possibility of a long-term relationship.

Nicole and Charlie had been dating for a few months. Nicole earned a meager salary working for a not-for-profit organization, while Charlie, who worked in sales, brought in a hefty income. He took her to up-scale restaurants and always picked up the bill. They'd have hot make out sessions in the car in front of her apartment building, but she wasn't ready to invite him upstairs. After four fancy dinners out Nicole began to feel that she "owed" Charlie, and should invite him in. She wanted to feel in a position of choice rather than feeling pressured into having sex by the imbalanced situation.

During a coaching session Nicole and I came up with a way to even the playing field. She loves to cook, and Charlie was delighted to accept her invitation to dinner - and even brought the wine! After they had enjoyed several of her wonderful home cooked meals, Nicole felt more balanced in the relationship, and when they did sleep together it was at her invitation.

Starting over encompasses getting in touch with your desires for intimacy. This is where the term "research" comes in. If you've had a lousy first date (something certainly never to be repeated), it's great research! This is a time for you to explore, to figure out what gives you pleasure. How will you know what to communicate to a partner if you don't know what you like?

Recipe for Starting the Dating Process

▶ The more you have in common with someone the easier it is to relate.

▶ Be clear about your criteria and preferences.

▶ Knowing and stating your boundaries is imperative. Remember that "No" can be a full sentence.

▶ If you choose to check out online dating, be sure your profile(s) represent you well. You might read through others' profiles for ideas and get help or feedback from friends or a coach.

▶ You've got a head start if you play golf, salsa dance, participate in a particular MeetUp group, go to church,

▶ Take him to a party with your friends. Ask your girlfriends for their honest assessment (very helpful if you're dazzled by strong chemistry!).

▶ Look your best.

▶ Meet in a public place-plan on coffee or a glass of wine for a short amount of time—leave wanting more!

▶ Consider hiring a coach to partner with you for your dating process.

▶ No matter how savvy you may be in your world, if you've been out of the dating loop for decades you may find yourself a beginner!

A Gourmet Recipe for Discovering Your Turn-On

When it comes to having a wonderful sex life, it all starts with knowing yourself and what you find pleasurable.

Please either sit or lie down comfortably, and imagine it's a lovely Saturday morning. You've just awakened from a restful night's sleep. You stretch, yawn and bound out of bed.

You've been looking forward to this day for weeks, as tonight you have a date with the most exciting, hottest guy you could have imagined. He meets all your criteria and then some. You can't even believe your luck!

He's planning to pick you up at 8:00 pm, and you've designed your whole day around getting ready for your big date. You're preparing delights for all your senses. First you luxuriate in a wonderful, fragranced bubble bath. After your bath you put on your favorite lotions and perfumes. You shave, style your hair just right and then you put on your makeup fastidiously, exactly the way you know it looks the best. Then you go to your closet and choose your favorite, accentuate-your-sparkly-eyes-and-your-curves clothing. You put on some beautiful music; might be soft rock or classical or perhaps your favorite jazz.

You take the wrapper off some of the best dark chocolate, which you pair with a delicious sherry and set them on the nightstand (or perhaps you'd prefer your favorite tequila, or simply lemonade). Conceivably, you have a mirror nearby so you will be able to watch the ensuing action. Incense or some flowers with a lovely scent like stargazer lilies or tuber roses grace your dresser. Then you wait. You feel and look amazing, and you are so turned on. You wait and you wait.

Then the phone rings. It's him, calling to say his plane has been delayed in another city due to a snowstorm. After swiftly moving through your initial and understandable disappointment, you surrender to the fact he won't be joining you after all your preparation.

But you know what? You're all ready. You're ready for the most delicious date of your life, and guess what? You get to be your own visiting dignitary. You now get to have a date with yourself. You've got the lights just right, or maybe it's candlelight. You've got your mirrors ready.

You might enjoy touching yourself with feathers, and having a beautiful glass wand or dildo that fits your yoni just right is a good thing. If you don't have a sexual lubricant on hand, coconut oil is wonderful.

Since you want to engage all senses including conceptual reality, a sexy story might be fun to read. Or maybe you just want to go online and find some raunchy, kinky stuff. Whatever turns you on; sample different things! Your brain is the biggest sex organ.

It's time to ask yourself what it is that gets you excited and you start exploring. Light touches with a feather and your hand follows with firmer ones.
You start discovering what you like by touching yourself as

you look in the mirror. You check in with yourself, "Am I getting engorged? Wet? If I touch this part of me, is it connecting with that part of me? Oooooh, that touch feels good....You feel yourself beginning the climb to orgasm.

It's feeling really good, but you don't let yourself have that orgasm yet. You realize how delicious you are and what a yummy evening you can have with yourself. You just learned something new; perhaps it's that spot behind your left knee that corresponds with another very androgynous zone. Or maybe you discovered something else that's just delicious. You realize, you wish there was somebody there that could kind of bite you sort of hard in the back of your shoulder...

And so your luscious evening comes to an end. You fall asleep with a smile on your face. You wake up the next morning, and it sure looks like a good time was had in your bedroom. Then you do some journaling about it.

What you've discovered are new ways that you find sensually pleasurable. Now all you have to do is be sure to convey what you like to the next lover that comes into your life. This might require taking steps to learn specific communication techniques that will serve you both in satisfying your desires, thus resulting in all around satisfaction.

Your job moving forward is to pay attention; to stay tuned to your pleasure! It's that simple. So when you do connect with a wonderful new partner you'll be able to communicate exactly what you desire and be gratified beyond expectation.

Seventh Course:
Get Your Sexy and Sassy On

Congruency – Putting all the Ingredients Together

You've done it; you've started over! Now that you've completed your past, it's time to live your life congruent to this new version of you.

- Does your lifestyle reflect who you're becoming now?
- Do you look the part?

Take an honest look at how you've immediately evaluated others within the first few seconds of meeting, and you'll be reminded that you're judged in the same way! Each of us forms perceptions based on the lenses of our unique experiences. As an image consultant, coach, speaker and seminar leader, I teach women and men how to show up in the world consistent with their level of expertise.

It is not enough to simply earn experience required to be an expert or leader in your field. If you want to be taken seriously, your physical presentation needs to be congruent with how you wish to be perceived.

Your clothing, posture, body language, hairstyle and smile are all means of communication. Any unusual aspect of how you look, speak or act, can distract from you being seen as a potential mate, expert or leader.

Consider these factors to be equally as important, if not more so, than what you have to say.

Generating Your Success Appeal

How you present yourself makes a statement. When in a position of looking for a partner, or leadership, you're more visible in the world; thus your choices are critical. Even what type of car you drive and the home you live in contribute to how others see you.

Consider how the world responds to the wardrobe selections made by Duchess Kate of Windsor, or the late Jackie Kennedy Onassis and all other First Ladies as well as rock stars, actresses and other cultural icons. Their clothing decisions influence and inspire fashion trends in our culture.

You've worked hard to transition out of the life that no longer serves you. Now, it's time to take yourself to the next level by mastering the following three C's:

- Clothing

- Confidence

- Charisma

Clothing and Style

"Beauty begins the moment you decide to be yourself" ~Coco Chanel

People form immediate opinions upon first seeing you. Since you do not get a second chance to make that great first impression, you must do it right the first time.

The clothing you wear should magnify your beauty. Yet if not well chosen, it can undermine your success. Deliberate, discerning style choices can enhance your ability to elicit the confidence required to earn the respect of others. When dating, you'll want to be sure you feel and look your most attractive.

How many times have you made a flash assumption based on what someone is wearing or how their hair is styled?

An important consideration is to dress in accordance with the venue, time of day and demographic of the people you're meeting. Former First Lady Michele Obama exemplified this. She wore haute couture dresses while hosting White House affairs. However, when she met with school children, she chose casual clothing from more affordable stores. I recommend you do research to determine the demographic of your client or audience. When it comes time and place to meet a date, the conversation you've had in advance can determine your wardrobe. It's no fun to find yourself inappropriately dressed. Do your homework!

My client Janice interviewed for a top-level executive position with a company specializing in high-end athletic gear. The company is managed and staffed by young, hip people in their 20s and 30s. Together we cultivated a more contemporary, fashion-forward style that resulted in Janice being more appropriately dressed. She got the position.

Linda, a skilled executive coach with an MBA, was in her mid-thirties when she came for assistance with her image. A lovely, petite, blonde-haired woman with an hourglass figure, she found herself not being taken seriously by her clients. It was necessary for her to present in a more mature and professional manner. This required a tailored wardrobe that engendered the respect required for her professional credibility. Given her proportions, and the fact that the eye tends to be drawn towards imbalances, we played down her shapely body and chose accessories that were understated and classic. Her transformation increased the level of confidence she needed to attract the business she wanted.

Both Linda and Janice's stories exemplify how changing your wardrobe can have a positive effect on self-confidence and on how others perceive you.

My client Barbara is a top software designer in the entertainment business. She went to Tokyo to present a new product to a number of prospects. Later she recounted what it was like to wait for her highly anticipated appointment with the head of Sony Entertainment.

"The walls were covered in autographed photos and memorabilia. Initially I felt insecure. Then, I looked down at my oh-so-stylish shoes and sleek, black leather portfolio and realized that even though I was nervous, I looked the part of the successful and creative software designer I am!"

As you can see, her confidence was renewed, and she completed her meeting with a new contract for her products.

Your Recipe for Looking Fabulous

▶ Dress according to your venue and target audience.

▶ Your clothing should showcase you, not scream for attention. Think of yourself as the artwork and your clothing as the frame.

▶ The eye is drawn toward imbalances. Dress to downplay any physical attribute that calls too much attention to itself.

▶ Wear your best colors to command attention, gain credibility and enhance your self-confidence. If you do not know which colors are best for you, consider hiring a color expert or an image consultant.

▶ Be prepared! Plan what you will wear in advance. Last minute surprises, such as a stain or rip, can be stressful.

▶ Footwear can make or break an outfit. Keep your shoes shined, well maintained and in style.

▶ Update your hairstyle; keep your cut and color current.

▶ Your accessories should complement your outfit, not overpower it.

▶ A great handbag or briefcase can complete your ensemble to perfection.

Confidence

Confidence is the belief in yourself, and plays a major role in how other people perceive you. Most successful leaders radiate self-confidence. They display assurance and evoke others' trust. They respect themselves and earn the respect of others because they emanate security and a sense of self-worth. They command attention and attract success. If you want to be credible as a leader, then your self-confidence is crucial.

"A good leader inspires people to have confidence in the leader. A great leader inspires people to have confidence in themselves." ~Eleanor Roosevelt, American, former first lady of the United States

You can change your life by developing confidence. When Sharon began her coaching relationship with me, she had just earned a master of business administration degree from Stanford University.

Though she had an excellent job in a leadership position at a financial institution, she didn't feel like the successful young woman she was. We worked on improving her level of confidence by putting the above tips, among others, into action.

After several months, Sharon wrote the following, "I'm still pinching myself at how radically different my life is today than it was a year ago. The serious investment I made in my working with you has paid off! Through eating a healthier diet and working out regularly, I have lost weight. In addition to being thinner and looking better, I have never felt stronger, more present or more powerful. I have entered into two of the best relationships I have ever had. The first is with myself, and the second is with a wonderful, spirited, life-loving man who has exceeded my expectations for how love can feel. We're moving in together next month!"

This concept translates easily to the dating realm. When you feel confident in your body, comfortable with your sexuality and you know you're looking good – you create more opportunities.

Charisma

As important as it is to dress appropriately and have self-confidence, it is the charisma or magnetism, charm and presence you emanate that will establish you as a person people want to know better, respect, and desire.

"Charisma is a sparkle in people that money can't buy. It's an invisible energy with visible effects."
~Marianne Williamson, American author, lecturer and activist

A charismatic leader has a natural ability to captivate and influence others. She radiates extraordinary power and inspires people with her appealing personality. When I think of charismatic people, I see individuals who are authentic with a remarkable ability to connect.

Recipe for Cultivating Your Confidence

▶ Confident people make good eye contact.

▶ They are prepared and put together in all ways.

▶ People with confidence radiate health and vitality. Most confident leaders are physically fit and feel good about their bodies

▶ They have a sense of humor and smile a lot.

▶ Self-confident people have good posture.

▶ They take responsibility for themselves in all aspects of their lives, both professional and personal.

▶ Confident people do not become defensive when receiving criticism. They listen to feedback and use it to evaluate their performance.

Lynne Twist, co-founder of The Pachamama Alliance and author of The Soul of Money, published by W. W. Norton & Company in 2006, is one of the most charismatic women I know. Her enthusiasm for the projects with which she is involved is contagious. When Lynne connects with you for even a moment, she makes you feel as though you are the only person in the room, even if she is addressing a crowd of thousands. In addition, Lynne's warmth, authenticity, compassion and ability to freely share her emotions serve her well as an internationally known fundraiser, speaker and author.

Bill Clinton, former president of the United States, combines his tremendous intellectual capacity with his enormous heart. He seems to connect with and enjoy every person he meets. He listens, and displays what looks like sincere and innate affection for people who are going through difficult times.

In Michael Ellsberg's book, The Power of Eye Contact, the author writes that people who experience Bill Clinton in person usually report that they feel like they are the only people in the room. According to Ellsberg, this is the transcendent power of eye contact. It is "… the ability to forge a connection so strong between humans, in so short a time, that two people feel like one in an instant. I know of no other force in human experience that can work such magic so quickly."

You might not be as naturally charismatic as Lynne Twist or President Clinton. However, you can certainly cultivate behaviors and actions that will empower your leadership style.

I have had the most intimate and lovely experiences with children and adults during my international travels, without necessarily exchanging a word. Particularly in Southeast Asia and Latin America I've noticed that both children and adults openly and unabashedly stare at me, fascinated by our differences. Here in the United States it's considered impolite to look people in the eye for more than a moment unless engaged in conversation. I've found it refreshing and enriching to connect with people in this simple way.

I have witnessed the power of eye contact and relational presence repeatedly during my years as a Speaking Circles® facilitator. In just a few minutes of standing in front of an audience, people can move through the emotions from shyness to fear to love as they allow themselves to simply see and be seen. A small, yet profound, action can generate huge results. If you are not accustomed to being with people in this way, I suggest you start making eye contact with your clients, friends, family members and even strangers. Do this until it becomes second nature.

Show Up in Your Radiance

Some confident, charismatic people were born with these characteristics. Others have learned how to develop them through practice and by working with coaches, consultants and mentors.

Immediately apply these compelling action steps and you'll be taken seriously. Your ability to relate to people authentically and personally will be enhanced. To improve your eye contact and communication skills, consider participating in a Speaking Circle. More information about Speaking Circles can be found at www.speakingcircles.com. Polish your image and presentation by hiring an expert image consultant or coach.

Accelerate your success appeal starting now. Which of the three C's—clothing, confidence and charisma needs attention? Take action to show up as the leader you are!

Sweet n' Spicy "To Do" List for Developing Charisma

Make and maintain good eye contact. When speaking to an individual or in front of an audience, take a deep breath, become aware of your feet on the ground and make eye contact with first one, then another two or three people without saying a word. The few seconds you commit to being quiet, rather than launching right into your presentation, will create a safe space for your audience. You will meet them in the silence.

These concepts are just as important for your personal life, especially if you're single and dating.

Communicate like a leader. Charismatic leaders naturally know how to relate to people and draw them in.

▶ Emulate these leaders by personalizing your presentations with stories and examples to which your audience can relate. This creates camaraderie and makes your message memorable.

▶ Address people by name to capture their attention and show your interest in them. The act of saying their name will help you re- member it.

▶ Give heartfelt compliments that give people a boost and help them feel good about themselves and you.

▶ Smile. A simple smile is one of the best and quickest ways of making yourself instantly more likeable and approach able.

▶ Oprah Winfrey is an excellent example of a leader who communicates using all of the above.

Some Sizzle for Your Overall Success Appeal:

Your clothing and style. Take an honest inventory of your physical appearance. When you intend to show up as a leader, be sure your style is congruent with your brand, and your clothing reflects your leadership role.

Your confidence. Be prepared, stand up straight, take a deep breath and project the level of confidence congruent with who you've become.

Your charisma. Powerful leaders differentiate themselves by connecting with people through eye contact, heartfelt compliments and genuine enthusiasm.

Dessert – A Dolce Take Away

You've had the opportunity to dive deeply into your past, clarified what's worked and what hasn't. You've designed aspects of what you want to bring into your life, and are rolling up your sleeves to start over.

Freedom was never your objective; as you knew from the beginning that it was your nature. Wings dry, you've untethered yourself from the imprisoning traditions and legacies. No longer are you forced to ask questions about what it is to be a woman. You've rebelled and won your freedom, and are now faced with an unknown, exciting territory. The maps have run out. The scripts are not written. The roles are no longer defined. What you are is what you make of yourself... today.

Together as free women, we create ourselves, as in no other time in history and no other place. This is our new beginning. Are you ready to claim what it takes for you to live your life, your way?

We both know the answer.

Glossary - A Language for Scrumptious Fulfillment

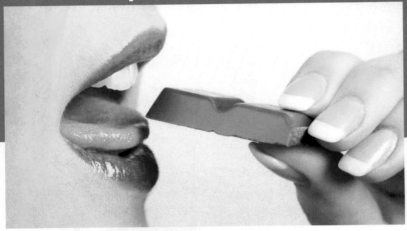

"Use the power of your word in the direction of truth and love." ~ Don Miguel Ruiz

There are lexicons, or vocabulary for all aspects of life. Every profession, sport, hobby, religion, etc. has its own vocabulary. Creating your sexy and sassy life requires a new way of speaking, in other words a new vocabulary or Lexicon. All of the words in this lexicon are English words with which you're familiar. They are included here to give you ways to focus energy in a more fun, fabulous and free direction. I invite you to be more deliberate with your use of language. The words we choose are powerful.

The following words are included here as they represent a subset of a more empowered vocabulary to support you in recreating yourself.

Andropause: A gradual decline in the production of androgenic hormones and especially testosterone in the human male, usually occurring during his forties or fifties. Also referred to as climacteric, male menopause. Symptoms can include depression, loss of libido, erectile dysfunction, and other physical and emotional symptoms.

Appetite: A strong desire or liking for something

"Sometimes it takes an overwhelming breakdown to have an undeniable breakthrough." ~ Unknown

Breakdown to Breakthrough

Breakdown: A physical, mental, or nervous collapse.

Breakthrough: A sudden advance especially in knowledge or technique: a person's first notable success.

Commitment: The state or quality of being dedicated to a cause, activity.

Congruent (congruency): The compliance between one's ideal self and one's actual self.

Now that you've redesigned your life, is your image congruent to how you wish to be perceived?

Content: information or experience provided to audience or end-users by publishers or media producers

Context: The set of circumstances or facts that surround a particular event or situation.

Criteria: A principle or standard by which something may be judged or decided

Desire: Wish, want, aspiration, inclination, impulse; yearning, longing, craving,

Drift State (state of being): A state of indecision or inaction. Tends to represent a "stuck" place.

Germinate: Come into existence and develop.

Hunger: Lack of food, emptiness, starvation, malnutrition.

Hunger and appetite (the distinction) Having an appetite is not the same as being hungry, nor is appetite about having a goal or intention. Goals can come out of our commitment to having your appetite fulfilled. Actions then get generated out of your commitments and goals.

Chances are you have the privilege of generating your life from your appetite, rather than from your hunger. Hunger is survival based, whereas appetite is generated from your desire, and is for pleasure.

IDK (I Don't Know) phase: Not necessarily comfortable, but certainly inevitable when going through any and all changes. Learn to embrace these times! They, too, shall pass.

Inertia: The tendency of a body at rest to remain at rest

Irresistible: Impossible to resist, having an overpowering appeal.

Magnetize: Attract strongly as if by a magnet.

Meaning: Implied or explicit significance.

"How you define a situation produces an emotional response and determines how you feel moving forward. Meaning equals emotions. Emotions equal life. Reshape your entire life by taking conscious control of the meaning you infuse in every interaction. Learn to harness your innate ability to supercharge your emotions, empower your decisions and elevate your life." ~ Tony Robbins

Menopause: the natural cessation of menstruation occurring usually between the ages of 45 and 55. Can be preceded and accompanied by symptoms such as hot flashes, mood swings, headaches, extra heavy or sporadic bleeding

Momentum: The driving force gained by the development of a process or course of events. (The context here is about how certain life style choices take on a momentum that sometimes require an intervention if they are no longer serving us.)

No Body = Nobody: Nourish and take care of your body- you only have one!

Perimenopause: The period around the onset of menopause that is often marked by various physical signs (as hot flashes and menstrual irregularity)

Pleasure: Happiness, delight, joy, gladness, glee, satisfaction, gratification, contentment, enjoyment, amusement, entertainment

Point Easy vs. Point Crisis: When we wait too long to make a necessary change, it can be hard and painful. However, "change can be easy" and is natural. Pain and dissonance are simply signals that it's time to make a change! (footnote: thanks to Diamond and River Jameson and the Total Integration Institute)

Pre-empt: To prevent (something from happening or taking place (forestall)

Preference: a greater liking for one alternative over another or others.

Refute: To expose as illogical, false, or incorrect.

Requirement: A necessary condition.

Research: Investigate, study, inquire into, probe, explore, analyze, examine.

Research is one of my favorite words! For example, in terms of dating and relationships, if you've had a wonderful time on a date; great! Consider that good research. If you've had a horrific date from hell experience, it was also good research! We learn from our pleasurable as well as not so pleasurable experiences. The date from hell and the yummiest date of your life are both great research!

Stranger: A friend you just haven't met yet

Truth: Veracity, truthfulness, sincerity, candor, honesty.

Unreasonable: Exceeding reasonable limits; exorbitant; immoderate

Righteous Stagnation: Justifiably stuck, stagnant

Stuck – Referring to its use in the context of being a victim. Thinking you are stuck in a situation rather than staying open to solutions

Vicissitude: A change of circumstances or fortune,

Victim mentality: An acquired (learned) personality trait in which a person tends to regard him or herself as a victim of the negative actions of others.

Wallowing – Staying stuck!

Stay away from using the following (disempowering) words! The examples in red are three less empowered ways to communicate, followed by more empowered examples in black.

Try – "I'll try to call you later."
Notice how saying you'll try to do something vs. saying you'll intend to do something mitigates the intention
More empowered: "I'll call you between 4:00 and 5:00."

Hope – "I hope you'll be able to make it".
More empowered: "You will be able to make it, won't you? I'd love to see you!

Kinda – "I'd kinda like to get together soon." (There's no commitment here!)

More empowered: "I'd love to get together. Let's make a date!

Addendum - Necessary Ingredients

Tips for Selecting Your Divorce Attorney

Selecting a lawyer to represent you in your divorce is more than just picking a name; it means establishing a close and sensitive relationship that will continue for months and perhaps years. It is important to find and hire the person who is right for you and your case.

Speak with others who have gone through it in the Sexy, Sassy & Starting Over! community website and events. Log on to www.SuccessAppeal.com for tasty references

Your state bar may have a process for certifying family law specialists and may give you names. The American Academy of Matrimonial Lawyers is an organization with a rigorous screening procedure which admits only qualified specialists. The American Bar Association and most local bar associations have family law sections.

Recipe for Selecting Your Divorce Attorney

1. Get names of lawyers from other professionals with whom you are working.

Lawyers, accountants, psychotherapists, members of the clergy and other professionals who meet and work with divorce lawyers can be a good source of referrals. A lawyer you already know and trust can be an exceptionally good referral source.

2. Get names of lawyers from organizations including:

-Your state bar certifies family law specialists

-The American Academy of Matrimonial Lawyers

The American Bar Association and most local bar associations have family law sections.

3. Get names of lawyers from referrals from other people who've gone through divorce.

Here are some criteria to consider:

1. Cost: Costs can vary significantly. It is best to interview several attorneys, as there are often highly skilled lawyers available who charge less but might not be as well known. Though some lawyers offer free consultations, beware that you are not simply being given a sales pitch.

2. Gender, age, race, religion, nationality: Irrespective of the lawyer's ability and experience, your comfort level is essential. If a common background is important to you follow your truth.

3. Credentials: There are objective factors that may help you evaluate the lawyer's professional competence and appropriateness. Take into consideration their membership and level of involvement with professional organizations. The length of time they've been in practice is important. Also, discover if they have published articles or books on family law. Do they teach other lawyers? All of these questions are indicators of experience, competence and reputation.

4. Personal Compatibility: The relationship between lawyer and client in divorce situations is especially important. You will be sharing intimate facts and the lawyer may have to give you advice that you may not like. Be sure the lawyer is a person with whom you can talk and feel heard. Trust your instinct! If you are not comfortable, trust your instinct and don't hire that person!

5. Location: It is beneficial and convenient to meet in person. Recipe for Interviewing your Lawyer Prior to Hiring 1- It's best to interview several lawyers (depending upon the urgency of your situation).

2- Tell them about your situation.

Have the following with you:

- A list of your assets, debts and sources of income
- A copay of the last several years tax returns

- A narrative or outline of the important events in your relationship with your spouse

- A list of things you want to discuss

3- Be prepared to audio record the interviews. "Rev" is a smartphone application that allows for recordings to easily be transcribed by people rather than robots. This will help you stay present, rather than distracted by note taking.

4- Specific questions to ask:

- What is likely to happen to me?
- How much property will I get?
- How much financial support can I expect?
- How much support will I have to pay?

- Do I have a choice of courts and does it make a difference?
- Are you easily reachable by phone/text?
- If you're not available, how will my call be handled?

- How much do you charge for the following: secretarial time, photocopies, postage, faxes, phone calls, supplies, computer work or any thing else other than your billable time?

- What expenses do you pay from the money I pay you and what do I have to pay directly?

- Under what circumstances would you refund all or part of my retainer fee?

- Do you have any personal feelings about the positions you would have to take if you represented me?

- How often are you out of the office in court, at conventions, on vacation and for other things?

- How do you cover my case at those times?

- How much do you know about the judge who will decide my case if it goes to trial?

- Do you think we can work together?

- Will you be available at the times that are convenient for me?

• Have you had experience dealing with cases like mine? Can you give me an example and tell me about the outcome?

Important Things to Know About Your Divorce

1. Alimony/Spousal support is almost always granted after a long-term marriage (minimum 10 years)

2. Retirement moneys will be cut in half, evenly.
3. If you keep the house, you're giving up something else. Keep in mind that houses come with property taxes, maintenance expenses and other costs. Keeping the house and giving up retirement savings or cash payments could put a person in a bind.

4. Your kids may be older but they might still be a factor. In many later life divorces, child support and visitation orders are out of the picture. However, that doesn't mean adult children aren't a consideration in the divorce proceedings.

5. Being bitter benefits no one, but there is no reason to be a buddy to your ex.

Remember you once loved one another! No matter how old you are, be as amicable as possible. There's no benefit in having contentious divorce. And, amicable doesn't mean being an open book. Sharing information such as future plans, desired assets, etc. could've a spouse considerable negotiating power during divorce proceedings. Be polite, be civil but keep it neutral and businesslike.

6. Make new friends, but remember that it's best not to start dating before your divorce is final. Depending upon your situation, dating too soon can upset children, anger the soon-to-be-ex-spouse, and add time and money to the proceedings.

7. Consider a prenuptial agreement for the second time around. Given that more second marriages are more likely to end in divorce than first ones, it's recommended to consider getting a prenuptial agreement.

Acknowledgements

Matt Morrison, Editor in Chief, and all things tactical!

"I couldn't have done this without him!" is an understatement. I am deeply grateful for Matt's remarkable ability to provide the riverbanks required to complete this project given the mercurial nature of the feminine. He's a man of his word. This, combined with his commitment, and rockin' sense of humor makes it a pleasure to do business together.

Leslie Hoffman, Photographer extraordinaire

Leslie is one of my favorite people and a rockstar photographer. Many friends and colleagues have commented that she's captured my essence in her photos.

Billy White

Billy's deep, abiding integrity set the foundation for our successful marriage and subsequent successful divorce. I have deep gratitude for Billy, my former husband and dear friend for life. I hope he appreciates the stories included here!

Bill Lamond

Bill's 'Pleasure of Business' course gave me specific tools that I have used consistently for over two decades. I'm grateful to Bill for the 'The Completion Process' included in this book. Also, his 'Fulfillment Based Language' concept inspired the glossary at the end of the book. I appreciate Bill's ongoing commitment to women leading from their pleasure and empowerment.

Diamond and River Jameson

Diamond and River came into my life just in time to help me navigate my mother's death when I was in my late 20's. Their authenticity to "walking their own talk" set a high standard for me. I'm grateful for their 'Point Easy to Point Crisis' model which is integrated into this book.

Margot Anand, Charles Muir, David Deida, Caroline Muir and Johanina Wikoff

It's been a privilege to study in depth with this list of illustrious teachers. Each is a pioneer in his or her own way, having written books and designed courses that have made a tremendous difference in the lives of thousands of fortunate people internationally.

Victor Baranco (posth.) and the staff at Lafayette Morehouse

Since the 1960's this extraordinary community of friends have lived with a commitment to the value of one another's pleasure and honest communication as the foundation of their lives together. Here in this book, I've gratefully included several communication modalities from my coursework. These include the 'Withhold Process', 'Appreciations' and 'The Training Cycle' (which I've renamed "A.R.T. Full Communication".

Fay Freed and the Cabro Community

My life changed for the better when Fay and her husband Ronn Landsman entered my life. At last I'd met my tribe! Our decades of enduring friendship as well as our business partnership has deepened and empowered who I am in the world. Fay is an example of a woman committed to her own pleasure as well as supporting other women to be in theirs as well.

Barry Morguelan, M.D. and the Energy for Success community

I appreciate Dr. Morguelan's commitment to both his allopathic practice as well as the ancient Chinese Energy system he generously shares. This system has allowed me to shift my focus from what doesn't work to what might be possible in any situation.

Shelli Heller

My transition from the Bay Area to San Diego County wouldn't have been the same without Shelli graciously extending herself to me. I'm grateful to my first San Diego County girlfriend for hosting me prior to assisting me in creating a home of my own here. She made my landing considerably softer than it might have been.

Yes Mastermind Group with Patrick Carney

I'm grateful for this extraordinary group of entrepreneurs with whom I collaborate weekly. It provides a consistent, mutually supportive network both professionally and personally

Wild Darlin's of Sebastopol and my Wonderful Friends

Thanks to this extraordinary group of West Sonoma County women who provided me a consistent grounding cord since 2000. Additional thanks to the contextual teachings of Diane Morrison, and to my friends Leslie King, Lani Jacobson, Becca Sandler, Laurie Javier, Merci Magdalena, Sally Churgel, Emily Bouchard, Teri Bigio, Debra Price Van Cleave and Madrone Styles, Kristen O'Hagen and Ross Kersey. I appreciate my new connections with Leslie Cady, Aria Ryan, Sylvia Becker-Hill, Karen Soriano and Jennifer Garland.

I am profoundly grateful to my sister Jeri Solomon, my dad Paul and stepmom Phyl Solomon. Their consistent encouragement and the knowledge that they have my back makes me one of the luckiest women on the planet.

Original Series Design: Matt Morrison/ Series Editor: Matt Morrison

Published by Success Appeal
5205 Avendia Encinas Ste A 92008
www.SuccessAppeal.com

Made in the USA
San Bernardino, CA
09 March 2017